THIS LOVE LIKE A RAGE WITHOUT ANGER

Bill Lewis 1978
Photo: Gloria Bousfield

THIS LOVE LIKE A RAGE WITHOUT ANGER

BILL LEWIS

POEMS 1975–2005

2019

First published by Colony Press in 2019
www.colony-arts.co.uk

Produced by The Choir Press

All rights reserved
Copyright © Bill Lewis 2019

The right of Bill Lewis to be identified as author of this work has been asserted in accordance with Section 77 of the Copyright, Designs and Patent Act 1988.

This book is sold subject to the condition that it shall not, by way of trade or otherwise, be lent, resold, hired out or otherwise circulated without the publisher's prior consent in any form or binding or cover other than that in which it is published and without a similar condition including this condition being imposed on the subsequent purchaser.

A CIP record for this book
is available from the British Library

ISBN: 978-1-9996948-0-7

Author's note

This book contains many of the poems published between 1975 and 2005. The selection has been hard to do as over the years many of my early poems were scrapped and the best lines from them used in other, better poems. Also, I had to decide which of my Medway poems to put back into my selected work. I had originally removed them because from 1992 to 1999 I was often reading in the USA and for the audience there it would have been like trying to watch a foreign language film without subtitles. I had tried in those poems to capture the voices of the region where I live by putting bits of overheard conversations into the poems and writing them in the estuary English in its Medway variation. Most of these are now back in print here.

This book is the first volume of my collected, and in this case, revised work. Most of my poems speak for themselves and I hate explanations but a brief note about my long poem *A Chilean Trinity* is necessary. I wrote the original version in Catalonia in the early 1980's but revised it by adding some lines in 2001 after the destruction of the World Trade Centre. I noticed that these two atrocities occurred on the same date thirty years apart and wanted to draw a parallel between the events.

I decided against putting the poems in chronological order but have tried to keep them in some kind of pattern (although this was not always possible). You will find work from my youth in rural Kent, The Medway Towns, Nicaragua, the USA, France and Spain. Also included are those written while working for the NHS at The West Kent General Hospital from 1978 to 1982. Almost all of the poems have been published in magazines or anthologies too numerous to mention here, but there are a few poems in this collection that were written in this period but which remained unpublished until this year.

CONTENTS

In Memory of Alan and Peggy Morris

Childhood

An apple, crisp
As Christmas day.

A massacre of
Stinging nettles.

Face tear webbed
In the playground.

Knowing the
Meaning of freedom

But not being
Able to spell it.

1975

Poems

With pen like a rod over pool of the page.
Waiting. Strange fish surface.

Four Minute Warning: A Poem For A Wife Who Works In London

I, who am in Chatham, love you
Who are at this moment in an
Office somewhere in London .
I tell this to my notebook as I
Sit alone in a crowded coffee bar
With its *formica* topped tables
And the scent of frying onions.
Where Punjabi business men talk
Launderettes and corner shops
And ashtray women suck on
Marlboros, smiling as deep frowns
Crease their foreheads, as they
Watch their snotnosed kids
Suck noisily on the straws of
Strawberry thick shakes.
I think, *What if they drop the*
Big One now? Will our last words
Be of nothing but burnt toast,
Failed alarm clocks and diatribes
against British Rail?
Looking out of the plate glass
At a pink jet trail in the winter sky
I write, *I love you. You who are*
More than four minutes away.

1982

Weight

A single tear
placed on a scale
weighs nothing

but in the heart it is as
heavy as a
mountain

1975

Haiku

Toffee factory. Night shift over
Air smells of mint, then banana.

1975

War Dream

My father's gun rends the silence
Puncturing the eardrum of the sky
Leaving my ears ringing.

A line of grey squirrels hang by their
Tails from the branch of a cherry tree.

I fall asleep in the grass and dream I am
Waiting for the sergeant to blow the
Whistle; a signal for us to go over the top
And be cut to pieces by shrapnel:
To die in the mud, entangled on devil wire.

I am ten years old and in my pyjamas
I should not be here, I cry. *It's a mistake.*

My father's gun rends the silence.

I wake and a line of dead soldiers in
Grey uniforms hang in the orchard.

1975

Six Things My Mother Said

1.
We had to have the council out to fix that tree,
That tree's got green atheists.

2.
Take off that wet shirt or you'll catch harmonium.

3.
He died of cancer of the sarcophagus.

4.
He ran in that London marrow bone.

5.
Poor thing he's one of those plastic children.

6.
We never had nothing. Nothing.

Strange that the only true thing she ever said
Was a double negative.

1982

My 1960s

Whenever someone mentioned
Simon Templar's name
A halo would appear above his head.

Adam Adamant never got arrested
For carrying an offensive weapon,
Despite walking around London with a
swordstick.

Captain Scarlet, *he's indestructible.*
But there were always strings attached.

Dr. Who was my grandfather and his
Companions were my true family.

I was 10 when I first entered the *TARDIS*
and 15 when I left school in 1968.

I couldn't wait to grow up and
Have adventures in the swinging Sixties.

One day I was stacking cans of beans
Into a promotional pyramid at *PRICERITE*

And it dawned on me that it was the 1970s;

I was not an international man of mystery;
I would not be asked to a mysterious
Country house and uncover a plot
By enemy agents who use mind control
Like John Steed did in an episode of
The Avengers.

I was a shelf-filler without any O or A levels.
In a winter of discontent peppered by power cuts.
It was the Seventies and my Sixties were over.

Dragonfly Skeletons

for Fliss

seasons
are dragonfly
skeletons
Frog resurrections
from once
frozen ponds

Lynton

for Maeve

In the middle of
The afternoon

The Herring Gull has
A fish shaped yawn

Dressed To Die

for my father

He always wore his cloth cap.
My mother would lift it
With one hand, while placing
His dinner in front of him
With the other.
He wore the uniform of
The rural working class:
A waistcoat (*Westcut*, he
                    pronounced it).
None of his shirts had collars.
When he went into hospital
He borrowed one of mine:
Pink with a flower power tie.
Well, it *was* the nineteen sixties.
It looked odd with his double
Breasted de-mob suit smelling
Of mothballs and jumble sales.
In the end both of the Big Cs
                    ganged up on him.
He was broken by
Cancer and Capitalism.
He died aged seventy three,
But one had begun to kill him
At birth, the other at seventy.
As far as I know it is too soon
To tell if there is a
Satisfactory cure for either.

Spells

Like a druid egg
Fossil stone
Found within
The walls of
A grassy mound.
Or an adder stone
To rub the eye,
Tell the cataracts
Good-bye.
Like the sowing
And hoeing
Of hemp seed on
Midsummer eve.
A benevolence
Of hawthorn
Blessing the
Cow shed door.
My father working
In the fields:
A scarecrow
Held together by
Sweat and straw.
My shaving mirror
Is a scrying glass
In which I see his
Weathered face.
Beneath the
Blank verse of
My urban eyes,
The rural rhyming
Past leaves a trace.

The Lookout Owl

Two-two Two-two, the lookout owl
Gives the game away to the game.

Two-two Two-two, there's clumsy
For you, they walk on two. Crashing
Through the thickening purple dusk,
Twigs cracking beneath size nine shoes.

Branches snap back at faces, skin shins.
We clods imagine ourselves quick
And quiet; but in truth our senses are
Flattened by a lack of need,

All stealth long ago civilised out of us
With broken guns hair triggered and
Barrels stuffed with leaves, our footfalls
Trip the early warning systems, the
Swivelling dishes of multi-directional ears.

Two-two Two-two, says the alarm and
Four legged forest folk hide in their hides,
                settle into setts and dark dens,
As if in air raid shelters deep
    waiting for the screech owl's *all clear*

1981

Weald

Above my head
The hawk and
Glider pilot both
Compete for the
Thermal lift
Of wheat.
I’m rolling drunk
From the river
Of mead and
The thick scented
Blood of the hop.

I am aged by
Norman church tower
And Oast alike.
As Countless Stones
Lay lost to a soft
Arithmetic of rain.

1983

This Love Like A Rage Without Anger

I touch the eye of your storm;
Kiss the hub of your turbulence.

The orchid of fire opens its petals
To the beak of the hummingbird.

Bodies shift against each other
                        like tectonic plates.

This love is a rage without anger,
It moved us in the way that
            some gods will dance with
A mountain and its peaks continue
Their choreography long after
                       the deity has passed.

This love is a rage without anger
There are other kinds of love I know

But for this poet it is the ink
      on every page of his notebook.

1983

Riddle Song

On the tree and in the tree
I climb the pain
Then down again.
On the tree and in the tree
Under rivulets of raven rain.
On the tree and in the tree
Raven's beak is in my eye
So tell me who am I?
So tell me who am I?
I am the Saxon and the Jew.
So tell me who am I?
I am the many and the few.
So tell me who am I ?
I am the one I am the three.
So tell me who am I?
I am the man I am the tree.
So tell me who am I?
I am the honey, hive and bee.
So tell me who am I?
I am the river, rain and sea.
So tell me who am I?
I am the three I am the nine.
So tell me who am I?
I am the bread I am the wine.
So tell me who am I?
So tell me who am I?

1991

The Sky Is In The Bird

I walk the road of feathers that runs
Into your thought's blue distance.

Feeling the whistling air between the
Tight economy of your fragile bones.

Now I know for sure, it is the poem
That writes the poet and the sky

Is in the bird or the bird could not fly.

1991

Against The Blue Wall of Heaven

Her island nestles against the
blue wall of heaven.

There are ziggurats of pink granite
with angels roosting in the upper tiers.

There are carvings of deities in the firmament,
Passages of dialogue collaged into the clouds.

If you look up at that sky, even for the briefest
moment, then back again,
The island will be gone,

And you will spend the rest of your life
trying to remember how it looked.

1982

Zeros

the lady talks to
dead drummers

I remember
when you
only sang for
wrist watches.

all of your lovers
were zeros.

except one
and he was
less than
nothing.

1980

Like Nomads

Like nomads
We cover much ground.
One day
It will cover us.

hobohemian

she’s a hobohemian
she wear oxfam dresses
she got red aztec feathers
she read manga comics
she swim mermaid forests
she got airtight garage
she got atomic moslem
she do helicopter dancing
she is a sexy scarecrow
she wears a homburg
                              in hamburg
she loves lino cut ladies
tasting chocolate lipstick
smoking black russians
she got aluminum suitcase
she is tattooed with tantra
she got tundra cheekbones
and just like new york city
she is deco by day
she is baroque by night
she is gotham gothic
she got clark kent glasses
she read the daily planet
she swears in litvak yiddish
shooting silver vodka bullet
at the back of her throat
and all my women friends
fall in love with her

1977

Margins

The word
Minority is
The biggest
Fiction
Of them all.

Soon there
Will be so
Many of us
Crammed
Together on
The edge

That the
Centre of
The page
will be
Blank.

Just a
Thick black
Border like a
Newspaper
Obituary.

1977

Un-Sonnet

It's about that sonnet that you've been
Working on for the last 50 years,

The one you started just after they
Liberated Auschwitz; or was it when
They dropped those 2 bombs on Japan?

You spent so long getting the meaning
To fit into the *abbaabba cdcddc*
Rhyme scheme that you never noticed
Vietnam or El Salvador happening.

When you were out I tore it up and
Threw the pieces into the fire. If I catch
You writing another, I'm going to impale
You on your own iambic pentameter.

1982

The Red Brick Racism of Walls

The wall said: *BLACKS OUT*,
in two foot high letters.
The wall opposite said:
Why are skinheads like bananas?

I don't know, said the first wall, *why?*

Because, said the second wall,
They're yellow and they hang around in bunches.

NATIONAL FRONT,
shouts the first wall.

SOCIALIST WORKERS PARTY,
the second wall yells back

DANGER ZONE, said the big yellow sign,
HARD HATS MUST BE WORN!

Written for *Rock Against Racism* 1980

It's One Of Those Parties Where Everyone Is A Writer Who Doesn't Write Or A Painter Who Doesn't Paint

You don't have to shove a loaded shotgun
in your mouth
to write great literature.
Nor do you have to fight bulls or hunt big game.
The only war you need to fight is the one that goes on
Inside of each and every one of us
each and every day.
No special clothing is needed.
Not even a famous blue raincoat,with a torn and
romantic lining.
If you make pictures you don't have to paint
Dead Greeks, Romans, naked screams or sunflowers
And the number of ears you have is optional.
You just have to paint and paint
and paint and if you have an
Eye that cares and a heart that listens,
There will be something at the end to show for all
the hard work (and it *is* work)
If it's any good, really good,
a lot of people won't like it.

1983

Conflict Observed

The man
Or woman,
Depending
On who's
Leaving,
Is throwing
Clothes into
A suitcase
And giving
All that
Jews and
Arabs stuff,
You know,
About oil
And water
Not mixing.
The woman
Or man,
Depending
On who's
Staying,
Is standing
In the doorway
Watching,
Arms folded,
Saying,
They had
Better mix,
In a desert
Economy
Both are
Essential.

Red Guitar *(for Victor Jara)*

My heart is
a red guitar
that your
disembodied
and once
crushed
hands
play.
I have
stored
up your
songs of
liberation
in my
soundbox
and now
I will
play them
LOUD to
wake this
subconscious subcontinent from its
nightmares, sending shivers down its spinal
column of a mountain range. My voice will
join the a capela choirs of *campesinos,*
Indians, priests, workers, nuns,
mothers and grandmothers of the
disappeared who gather in
the central squares of capital cities.
All those who have loved and by definition
suffered. These songs contain the soul
of the drum and the *siku* pipe, these songs
contain the laughter of crimson cockatoos
from the rainforests of all our interiors.
My heart is a red guitar. Your fingers
dance over my steel-wound
strings like cayenne
sparks.

A Chilean Trinity

1)
You are the child
Who mastered
The art of the rain
And became
Slave to its truth.
Everything that is
Organic and tellurian
Is made incandescent
By you and collected
In cages of ink.
Searching the forests
Of the south
For buried honey or
Spiders fashioned
From soft rubies.
69 scorched earth summers
Knit themselves
Into your bones.
Six perfect raindrops
You kept in a match box,
How you wept when
They turned them
Into seven daggers.

2)
Many came seeking different
Kinds of treasure in that
Leaf fragmented light.
In 1549 the Crown of Spain
Proclaimed Valdivia Governor.
He, like all the plunderers, hunted
Gold ruthlessly, with a
Desperation as if it would
give him eternal life,

Until he was captured by the
Araucanian Indians who made
Him a gift of what
he most desired
by pouring it in its
Molten state into his mouth.

3)
Pablo, I have visited the Spain of
Your heart, where the spirit of
Lorca stands like a
beautiful flamenco dancer
in front of a firing squad.
She wants to sing them her latest songs
But they just want to see her legs
perfect and Arabian beneath
Her gypsy dress before they open fire
Machismo will always be the
Greatest enemy of the Revolution.

I have visited the Spain of your heart.
The bulls still run in Pamplona and
Blind vendors still sell lottery tickets.
A customer buys two and pins one on
The seller's lapel. For luck. Rather a
Moorish custom, this far north,
But then, in the Bull Rings all over
Catholic Spain you will hear the name
Of Allah invoked in every *Olé.*
There I saw an old man wearing a
Black beret and a face borrowed from
Picasso, sitting in a bar with a glass of
Pale sherry in front of him, the past
Reflected on its surface, his face a
Leather wallet, in which he carried a
Sepia snapshot of the lost Republic,
Where the ghostly airforce of reaction
Forever flattens the holy cities of hope.

In Barcelona I walked the *Ramblas,*
A mad dog Englishman at siesta time
When the stalls that sell newspapers,
Flowers, pornography, livestock and
Magical realism are closed and the
Whores come out, the tired stars of noon.
It was two days before the Fiesta
And the worst rain in years had damaged
Many of the decorations. In the plaza
A flying demon, with a bright orange penis,
Strung between two wet palm fronds;
The falling torrent had smashed holes
Through his balsa wood and canvas wings;
A prostitute sheltered beneath a giant figure
Of Christopher Columbus, passing the time
By filling in a pocket crossword book
With the stub of an eyebrow pencil.

But, Pablo, there is much you would
Love here in this Spain, with its democracy
So new that you can smell the ink
                    (*in my pocket pesetas jingled.*
Some with the face of King Juan Carlos,
Others with that of The General,
                    all mixed up together).

Guernica hangs in Madrid and still, in
Those streets, proud women with eyes
Like black butter that can melt the sun
Walk beneath wrought iron balconies,
Where caged birds sing their thousand
Bright yellow songs.

4)
I have visited the Spain of your heart
But I have been never to your own
Homeland, where you sleep but do not rest.
Chile, land of seemingly irreconcilable
Differences, laying beneath a white

Antarctic star set in a cobalt blue flag
Of a sky, while beneath it, under the
Crimson field, its miners work the
Salvation of rock, their faces and
Eyelashes powdered with nitrate,
Glistening bodies veined with
seams of copper.
Chile, where not even the last Prussian
Army in the world can silence the guitar
Music, red, green and eternal that rises
From the *poblacións,* beating
Cueca rhythms off the surface of the moon.

Valparaiso, where the southern Atlantic
Wind beats rain into the shanty towns
Threatening to silence the red clocks
That tick in the sea chests of sea dogs.
A cold rain whose droplets stick to
The cheap woollens of the street urchins.
Where golden widows cover their
Seaweed hair with black lace mantillas,
Where a priceless Stradivarius violin
Sprouts wings and flies
To the pawnbrokers of the north.

5)
The small boy holding his father's hand
Asks, What is that place?
That's the Marine Infantry Barracks, my son,
Where they took us blindfolded. It was a
Place of pain and electricity.
We called it The Laughter Place.
And what is that painting on the wall?
That is a mural for Popular Unity, my son
Still there after all these years.
They'll never scrub it off.
Why not Papa?
Because we pissed in the paint, it seemed
To make it stick to the wall better.

6)
I am old enough to remember
Another 9/11, years before
The Twin Towers of
          the World Trade Centre
Were destroyed.
When it was the USA that was
Culpable. On
That other 9/11
The rest of the world looked
The other way and stuffed fingers
In its ears, so as not to hear
                    the cries.
Pablo, that was when you left us.

When the army held up your
Ambulance as you were rushed
          to the hospital.
A sky filled with
                    counterfeit eagles.

When they murdered Allende
They said it was suicide.
But we all know how easy it is
To shoot yourself in the
Back of the head with a machine gun.

The gun was a gift from Castro,
Inscribed, *For Salvador from*
His Comrade in arms, Fidel.
If by suicide they meant he
Tried to create a fairer society
To thwart the bloated desires
Of the copper bosses,
Multi-National Corporations
                    and the CIA
Then it was a suicide,
But only of a metaphorical kind.
Literally it was murder.

Who were the accomplices?
One for instance, was a
Manufacturer of toothpaste,
Another a distributor
of toilet tissue.
One wore a white but plastic smile.
Another's words were not
worth the paper
They were smeared on.
That was over 30 years ago
but each 9/11 is connected
By the same thread
And at its root a beast whose
Name is Legion,
whose name is Corporate.

7)
Pablo, last night I saw Che.
He was smoking an emerald cicada.
His hands were in Cuba
But his heart beat beneath
The ribs of many young
People in the old hills of many
Young and ancient nations.
And in Peru and Nicaragua
In Brazil and Argentina
There are priests
(Not the narrow men in god collars
Who speak the dogma of dog and
Called you excommunicate)
But others who see a God
Behind the Dialectics of nature
And live the phrase,
On Earth as it is in Heaven.
Pablo, when they ask did it end
With a bunch of aged Comrades
Singing the International
On some rainy Santiago afternoon?

I say no, because you have been seen
Walking arm in arm
With your Compañero President
On one side and on the other

The Young Singer
                    of Unfinished Love

Neruda.   *Allende.*
            Jara.

Such a very Chilean trinity.
When the crowd became the music to
Your lyric and in the benign hatred
Of armoured cars, they stood in defiance
Against the Midwives of Death.

Spain, 1982 revised after 9/11/2001

Moon Hare

Moon-full and still a little March-mad
Under the first full moon of April
The brown hare made white by
                    reflected luna light

A Stolen crucifix in its mouth, trailing
Rosary beads behind it like debris
In a comet's tail as it dashes through

The long grass, fast in fear that the moon
Lady might split its lip with a silver axe.

2004

The Sky Clad Christ

I am the pagan Christ,
sky clad and cloudless.
Ploughed into the
primal scripture of nature.

Nobody sees the Creator
until they first look at the creation.
Nobody gets to the parent
unless they take the child by the hand.

I am the sweet silage of summer past,
stored in silos, that sustains
cattle in the cold months.

I am the pagan Christ,
a corn doll sacrifice, thorn pinned
to the harvest yet to come;
The June nights
captured in dark pools of shadow
beneath the apple trees.
I am the hunter,
owl-feather wise and fox-brush crafty

I am also the hunted,
red breasted and broken,
Like the blue horizon is broken by
woods and water towers.

I am the Pagan Christ
Sky clad and cloudless.
I come before language.

I am the author written into the
green book of the grass,
the primal scripture.
It is easier for the illiterate
to read me than any scholar.

I am the metaphor made flesh
so you may know that:
All flesh is metaphor.

1991

Apple Stars

Instead of the usual Arctic to Antarctic slice
Let the knife circumnavigate the equator.

When you look inside each hemisphere
You'll find a perfect pentacle at the core.

Standing in an orchard you imagine the
Hidden constellations in the crisp fruit flesh.

Trains Of Thought

The moon is a cold ten pence piece.
The men wait for the train that is late.
The 5:32 from Chatham to Maidstone.

Their destination is written in white
Letters on the back of their donkey jackets.

Their hands are balls of rope;
                    blue knuckled and gripless.

★

One of us yawns and the train comes crashing
Out of his mouth.

He loses several teeth.

We manual workers, some skilled, others not,
Are men of Kent or Kentish men
Depending on which side of the river we
Began this journey.
We built The Victory at number one dock.
We fixed Rochester Bridge to the sky
With white hot rivets.
We cut the Cathedral from
                    Kentish rag-stone
And you still see the rhythm of our work songs
On its hard face.
Our lives are cut from the chalk of the
                    North Downs,
Our faces sandblasted from

Concrete, our hair falls
on our shoulders like cement dust.

Our lives are cut from chalk like the
Tunnel this train must enter.
We are Kentish men and men of Kent
Even the Asian amongst us who,
Like Saxon and Norman before them
Are just another layer on our
Genetic journey.
They may pray in
Urdu or Arabic but it's Anglo-Saxon
when they swear.

There are those of course who believe
In the purity of our language
But the fact is that each wave of immigrants
Gave us new and useful words
Making English the only language that
Needs a thesaurus.
I use *shampoo*. I drink *tea.*
My wife's aunt lives in a *bungalow*
I wear *pyjamas* in the winter
I wear *clobber*. Eat *Nosh.*
I sometimes eat a *curry*
I never buy *schmatta.*
I can be *ill* via the Vikings, *sick* from the Saxons
and even have a *Malady*
courtesy of the Normans.
So nice to feel impure.
The language that does not change is dead.
You won't find any new
variations of Latin or Sanskrit.
Assimilation is a two-way journey.

★

We were never masters of the English language.
We were its slaves and like all slaves,
We were bad workmen.
Always looking for a chance to shave the end
Off a word; drop a spanner in the
collected works;
Drop a fragile letter on the shop floor.

We are Kentish Men or Men of Kent
This is not a sexist comment as there are few
Kentish Maids or Maids of Kent
On the 5:32 to Maidstone. It will be another
Three hours before the white-collar workers
Fill the platforms for their daily commute.
Today the only females in this carriage
Are the one tattooed on the arm of the man
Opposite me and the one with a staple
Through her belly on page 3 of his ***SUN***
That he is looking at with a mixture of
desire, disgust and …fear?
The journey is longer for some than others.

We pass mountains of scrap metal.
Dockyard crane transformed by moon light
into steel brontosaurus,
the jet plane above a pterodactyl.
Not far from here they say Caesar crossed
The Medway, some say with his
war elephants.

★

In the distance across the mud flats
Between the Medway City Estate and St. Mary's Island
Where once the skies were filled with flak,
Phantom *ak-ak* guns *ak-ak* again.
Or is it the sound of a motorbike distorted by the river?

★

We hurtle across Rochester Bridge
Steel girders strobe the moon, and below us
A green starboard light turns the Medway
to the river Styx.
None of us know or want to know
the engine driver's name.

At Cuxton we pass the cement works
Every inch of it covered in pale dust,
From corrugated roof to the logs
in the timber yard next door.
Windows stare their milky gaze
Like an old man in the final stages of glaucoma.
A night mirage of industrial gothic,
DAZ white in the not quite morning light.

At Maidstone the gas works has its own sunrise
Rust red at the bottom, cobalt blue at the top.

★

It was in this town in more radical times
Kentish Rebels commanded by Watt Tyler
(a medieval Che Guevara)
Stormed the Archbishop's palace to set free
John Ball (a forerunner of today's
Liberation Theologians)
before marching on London.
For all of Adam's delving and Eve's spinning
We are still ruled by the same masters;
only the names have changed.

★

At Maidstone West the train thunders from the tunnel
Not like a tear from the eye of a Cyclops,
only a poet would tell such a lie,
But like a train from a tunnel.

★

This is Maidstone. On leaving the train please ensure you
have all of your belongings with you.
Please mind the gap between
Your expectations and
what is actually going to happen.

★

Due to the cold weather the train has
difficulty gripping the track
causing pseudo lightning and
choirs of metallic voices
sing from the wheel rims,
with words only audible to the
mad or the divine,
illuminating the platform with
showers of blue sparks.

Chatham and Maidstone 1982
Revised and enlarged 2005

In Chatham High Street

I wander without aim letting the town
Soak into me like rain. My eye takes
In the *faux* Babylonian patterns on
DIXONS upper windows and the Art Deco
Stylised elephant frieze that runs
        the length of BURTONS the tailors.

There is no time in this poem. I have
Walked in it for years but it always seems
Like the same day; year; decade.
The poem is airtight and its contents
Preserved from going stale and decaying.

The coursing crowd with its clash of
Colours: sunlight on bright blue denim
Dazzles the eye: the mix of punk rock
Pink and day-glo green, Mohican haircuts,

Purple saris, white turbans, West African
Women in oranges and yellows, their
Cotton dresses with bold ethnic prints.
Muslim men in white caps pass
Art students in retro tweeds and pork pie
Hats or black berets bought from OXFAM.

Busking Medway musicians in black
Leather jackets playing electric guitars,
One slapping a tea chest bass outside
ALDERS Department store, as they
Render a passable version of
The Singing Loins: *Chatham Girls.*

                    Real Chatham girls
Wearing jointed gold clown medallions,
Romany style hooped earrings and
Attitudes borrowed from last night's
                episode of '*Enders*

Overweight people wearing sports
Clothing and trainers that they could
Never run in rub shoulders with ex *mateys,*
With battleship grey hair, exiled from
HM Dockyard Chatham by time and closures.

These are my people.
They don't know it yet
But they just can't wait to get
on to the pages of my book.

Bus Station Fragments

As I wait I hear passing
Snippets of conversation:
The skeleton of a kite is
A restrained crossbow.
What? I turn but they
Are now out of earshot.

A man tells his wife,
John is a frightened man.
He says this with some
Menace and I wonder if
John might fear him most.
I also hear a woman say:
That Colin is one of
            them cycle paths.

While I am still imagining
This, another man says
To the person walking
With him: *so what did you do*
When you were still alive?
I don't hear the reply, as the
101 arrives and I get on.

Audio Tape

He mimes it with
His hands while
          telling me.

Turning his index
Finger in a
Winding motion.

I got there just
In time, he says,

Her talking book
Had come unspoken.

1980

Headlines

Medway man in ram raid terror!

★

Medway man in four lane pile up!

★

Medway man in major drugs bust!

★

Medway man in warehouse inferno!

★

Medway man wins lottery jackpot!

★

Medway man lost on Falklands!

★

Medway man held in murder case!

★

Medway man's secret life!

The Medway Suite

1.
The town is a commonplace book,
                                        a common
                              place book

These streets are a *book of invasions,*
A dictionary of surrealism,

An illustrated history of concrete and cement,
A pulp fiction, a user's manual,

A graphic novel in 3D, a forbidden Grimoire,
A pop-up picture book, a book of crosswords,

A bumper book of facts, a romance,
A bodice ripper, a Bible.

We are neither the salt of the earth
Nor the scum that floats on the surface.

These are our streets.

We are wise and stupid, prosaic and poetic,

Generous and bigoted, in the
          same breath in the same sentence.

The town is a commonplace book,
                                        a common
                              place book.

There are voices in the empty street.

2.

...It's no good Doctor I've still got me chest...

...well, I stopped watching it, it had language...

...I told her you ain't ugly enough to be beautiful...

... I woz everywhere like the weather
an she woz all over me like a cheap suit...

...we always get some kind of weather this time of the year
...e sed make it a bit good
an I did an e woz well pleased...

...as for the parents, she woz neither
use nor ornament to them...

...poor bloke e gets them imaginations...

...praps it woz just a phrase she was going fru...

... she could draw luvely photos though...

... short staffed today
so you gotta be in like flyn and on it like a bonnit

...see ya wouldn't want to be ya ...

... laters...
... laters ... ... laters ...

3.
There are voices in the empty street,
some slid into my notebooks
and waited there to be reborn.

Not just in my notebooks,
Sometimes on the back of receipts,
paper bags, in the margins
of takeaway menus,
even bus tickets.

Sometimes the ink had faded
and I had to strain
to hear the faint voice.

4.
The assistant in the flower shop
Looks out at the woman passing

In the street and clocks that
She is wearing clown makeup,

A man's suit and a bowler hat,

Blimey, who let her out?

Then she adds,

Tell you what, if you stand here long
Enough you'll see yourself walk past.

5.
In the queue a woman is telling
Someone about her father's funeral,

He liked to read. Friction mainly.
We got him a nice headstone, it was

Shaped like a stone book and
It looked real
        but you couldn't turn the pages

He liked dogs too but they
            never 'ad no stone dog.

6.
The woman in WH Smith,
                        telling her sister:
You've gotta stop letting
People brow beat you!

You gotta stop letting them
Push you from pillar to post!

You're too soft! Do you know that?

You shouldn't do things just
Because someone tells you to do it!

You really shouldn't!

You gotta...
          are you listening to me?

You're not even listening to me!

7.
June 1667 and Samuel Pepys' quill
Scratches words on the page of his diary:

Up; and news brought us that,
The Dutch are come up as high as the Nore;
and more pressing orders for fireships.

June 1987, I walk across the Field of Fire,
Between Chatham and Gillingham,

Kept clear of houses so the big guns could
Blast a French invasion that never came.

Gillingham is at a higher elevation and
Chatham seems to rise up as I get closer.

A Peregrine falcon, one of a pair that
Nest in the chalk cliff at Fort Amhurst,
Circles the escarpment searching for prey.

The War memorial thrusts up into
The cloudless sky like a stone rocket ship.

The Dockyard Matey who told me: *This was*
During the war when I was just an apprentice.

There was this one air raid when a ship
Made it out of the dock but it took a direct hit.

I wanted to help but the foreman said, No
It's a real hosepipe job. The deck's like a

Butcher's shop without the sawdust.

8.
Two swaggering shirtless youths,
The sweet pungent smell of *ganja*
Following them like a blue ghost.

One of them has a dotted line
Tattooed around his neck with
The words CUT HERE in red letters.

As they pass, I catch a snippet of
Their conversation along with the
Aroma of cheap aftershave and *Skunk.*

Bruv, I only got nicked by der Filth
And I 'ad some gear on me so I

Swallows it and spent the next two
Nights banged up, hoping it wouldn't

Go through me until I was out.
Luckily I was constipated and didn't

Manage to crap until after me Brief
Got me bail, which woz a bit

Andy'arry coz I wouldn't av liked
Swallowing it for a second time.

9.
The woman on the 164 speaking to her friend,
Who's sitting three seats away,

loud enough for every passenger to hear:

I'm going under the knife tomorrow.

I am having the lot taken out.
Well, I don't need it anymore, do I?

If only it was as easy to get rid of me old man.

He's me third and none of them were any good.

10.
In the canteen Jill tells Vi and Elsie:

I told him if you go and get yourself
Killed on that motorbike, don't bother
Coming home coz
I'll murder you.

I don't know why you are all laughing
coz I bloody mean it.

11.
Vi telling Jill in on their ciggie break:

'E stands on me doorstep wiv 'is
Woolworfs earring and his cheap suit
Telling me it don't cost nuffink,
not a penny.
It's totally free,
Then e sez,
you jus' pay
a liddle bit each mumf.

Ooh I wanted to slap him silly.

12.
The woman in Singh's Mini Mart who is
Talking to her friend as she is being served:

Never mind Joan, it wouldn't have lived.
Blood everywhere there was and two of
Them jam doughnuts please Mrs Singh.

13. (for Michael Horovitz)

The town is a commonplace book,
a common
place book.

Where poets walk in streets named after ships
and battles.
walking on history.
Zion-hearted,
Oak-hearted.
sometimes Dickensiandark,
Anglo-saxophoned
and punkrocked
Medway.

I stand, notebook at the ready,

Unconverted amongst the high street
cash-converters
in the bright Blakeian morning

14.

I still hear those voices in an empty street,
although they mutate with time,

The wheel of vowels turning still
until estuary English morphs into *Jafaken*

and perhaps pseudo-Slavic,
by way of Euro rap.

Talking text with a dash of Romani,

ClockworkOranged

in an oh so Kentish
RiddleyWalkered way.

Five towns moving slowly toward
becoming one city.

The river running through them
like a wet razor.
As it weaves its way
it slices letters off the ends of words.

Envoi

Dear Bill Lewis, thanks for letting
me read some of your poems. They was

Good. Some of them was funny. Me and
my boyfriend had trouble reading them

at first but then we read them out loud
and realised they was written in Chathamese.

Funny I speak that way but have trouble
reading it yet I can read proper English

but I don't speak that way. Yours Donna xx

Café Poem

You will find me in
One of my many
Offices: a cafe without
An accent over its E.

The light bulb
Forty watt and naked.
My notebook full of
Coffee fuelled scribble.
After the next cup
I will be flat broke
But so far unbroken.

On the menu board
The white magnetic
Letter N has fallen
From the *Stewed Mince,*
Causing some alarm
But possibly
        not inaccurate.

Greasy Spoon

All writers are stool pigeons.
Don't sit next to me in a café
Unless you're prepared to find
Your words in one of my poems.

Take those two men who just
Came in, and have ordered
Their full English from
Stella the waitress.

One of them is complaining
About his eldest boy:
The little toerag is only
Tooled up in the playground
And shivs one of his mates,
Not bad, just a scratch like.
I had to slip his parents a
Monkey each to wipe their mouths.
That's what I get for sending him
To a posh school.
Costs me a packet in fees.

Stella arrives with their plates.
She is wearing a pink bandana.
One of the men says: *What's*
Up with your neck, luv?
You been having it off with
A vacuum cleaner or something?
Stella's face goes the
Colour of her scarf.
She knows that love bites.

The two men laugh as if they have
Just outdone Noel Coward
For witty repartee and

Go back to the conversation:
I blame those lefty bloody teachers.
Bloody teachers, says one of them.
The perfect father replies:
I told him you cut this violence out
Or I'll kick the living shit out of you!
They eat until their egg and
Brown sauce smeared plates
Look like edible Jackson Pollocks.
Out of the corner of their eye
They see my pen move
Over the page and go schtum.

1985

In The Imagined Medway Night

The wind runs through the whisky sick night
Like a headless chicken,
Beating black rain into the steep heights
Of the house clad hills;
Gusting along the high street, hammering
The lion headed doorknocker of the
Tattoo studio and scattering empty
Crisp packets, that flap like cartoon ghosts;
Blowing along Intra, past the sex shop and
The synagogue and
                    pubs with nautical names.
The dark wind blows through
The ruined Norman Keep, without
Paying the four quid entrance fee,
Howling as it rises in the floorless shell,
The roaring penetrates the Cathedral
Where god dreams of floods, rainbows,
White spume of storm coloured seas
Shaping and re-shaping into the forms of
Mermaids, gryphons, unicorns and other
Beasts, not wanted on the voyage.
The wind runs through the imagined night,
And the dreams of Edwin Drood,
Charles Dickens and the sleeping souls of
Troy Town, as they turn in their warm
Posture sprung beds, casting wishes like
Unscratched scratch cards and un-bought
Lottery tickets off Blue Boar Pier,
Sun Pier and Thunderbolt Pier.
                          Somewhere between
Chatham Reach and Limehouse Reach,

In water too shallow for it to be possible,
A ghost submarine becomes visible,
Whilst the seven thousand year old
Medway Bog Man
(which, according to local
Historian, William Loveday, once resided in
A glass case in the Guildhall museum until
He disappeared during an air raid in 1940)
Opens his peat-packed Mouth and sings.

Poem for Billy Childish

A typical day and the city is
Busy creating poets
                    in its own image.
And the poets are also
Busy creating the city in
                      their own image.
In May Road, Rochester
                    Mr. Billy Childish
        (aged 27 and ½)
Dyslexic,
Attacks his typewriter,
                which also suffers from
Dyslexia,
                which also suffers…
While outside
               two stray mongrel dogs
Try to rip out
               each other's throats
And in the clear blue sky

The big yellow sun shines like an
Illustration in a child's picture book.

1987

The Rubaiyat of a British Rail Worker

The stone is flung.
The stars have flown.
Ibrahim wakes alone.

No Sultan's Turret
In a noose of light
Shines outside;

Just a cold and rainy
Bike ride that will

Without fail get him
To work at *British Rail.*

The bird outside
The window maybe
A cockney *sparra*

But the song it sings for
Ibrahim is, *I begin*
*With name of Allah.**

**inspired by a piece of Arabic calligraphy where the end phrase of the poem is in the shape of a bird.*

Airmail From Brazil (song lyrics)

She wears a charm around her neck
Sent airmail from Brazil.
Blessed by a *Macumba* priestess
With the power to heal or kill.
See her walk the streets of Paris
And in the Bois du Boulogne.
Selling the night her cinnamon skin
When the moon's like a silver coin.
Airmail from Brazil,
   Airmail from Brazil,
      She wears a charm around her neck
         Sent airmail from Brazil.

Mother church and *Macumba*
Both have their appeal,
But on the underside of midnight
Who's to say what's real.
See her sipping fizzy soda
In some red light bar.
Watched over and protected
By the spirit of a jaguar.
Airmail from Brazil,
   Airmail from Brazil,
      She wears a charm around her neck
         Sent airmail from Brazil.

There's a doctor who lives in Thailand
Who she needs to pay
If she wants to be a woman
On that dreamed of future day.
She needs all the help she can get
Six foot tall in her shoeless feet.
Handcuffed to her birth certificate
Let the *macumba* drum beat.
Airmail from Brazil,
Airmail from Brazil,
She wears a charm around her neck
Sent airmail from Brazil.

Sometimes it seems that black is white
And the night is day.
But they say that in the twilight
Every cat is grey.
She knows a few women's secrets
Though the cops all call her a fag.
That all the saints are made of plaster
They're just African gods in drag.
Airmail from Brazil,
Airmail from Brazil,
She wears a charm around her neck
Sent airmail from Brazil.

Written for the band *Ghost Dancers* 1986

Biker Aesthetic

Biker woman in Railway Street
Channeling rock chick attitude

On the back of her jacket in metal
Studs: KAWASAKI Z 1000

In the hip pocket of her *S T R E T C H*
Denim jeans a steel comb dances

1979

Rose

She razors a red rose.
It bleeds Shakespeare juice.

1982

Hair Cut

Outside, the red and white
Striped pole travels to infinity.

Inside, the floor grows a full
Beard at an alarming rate.

The man in the chair is
Saying, *The trouble with*

That Mick is short arms
And deep pockets,
Especially when it's his round.

He reckoned it was the flu but
I think it was drinking out of
Wet glasses that made him sick.

The barber shaves the man's
Neck, and says, *and as for that*

New shopping centre, there it
Stands with all the grace of
A turd in a bowl of custard.

1979

gun dan tan eni

gun dan tan en i
dan der tan
How. Now. Down. Town.
dan der
pand shop
arand a pand
pand land
der pand in
yer pockit.
dan giv me ten
dan giv me five
it's all yours
fer two fifty
put yer money
away luv it a'int
no good ere coz
i'm givin' it away
i'm a nutter
i'm mental
i must be
coz I'm givin'
it away
cutting me
own froat
it's like
takin candy from
a baby en it
yer robbin' me
blind, blind.
it's a mad 'ouse
i don't care.
i jus don't care.
mix it all up
eny where yer like
two fer der

price of one
i sed put yer
purse away luv
i'm givin' it away
givin' it some
of dis
givin' it some
of dat
givin' it
de old wun two
givin' it de
old heave ho
givin' it de
old soldier
givin' it de
old ows yer farver
givin' it away
every fings
a pand
der pand in
yer pockit
der pand in
yer 'and
pand fer pand
the latest
the best
original artists
ten percent
less fat
for a limited
period only
as seen on TV
cut yer bills
in 'arf
jus two more
great weeks
prices slashed

it could be YOU
it could BE you
it COULD be you
IT could be you
double points
on all dese items
last years?
no guv
when I said
last years
i mean it
woz last year's
not it will
last you years
no refunds
no names
no pack drill
no licence plates
no tax
no guarantees
no way José
no sell by dates
no use by dates
no consume
by dates
no nuffink.

Rochester Market 1983

School Story

den ‘e fighted him

No Johnny, he didn’t.

yes ‘e did miss
‘e fighted him

No Johnny, he fought him.
Fought him.

‘e didn’t fink nothing miss
‘e hit im wiv an ‘ammer.

School Story 2

—How does Tracey
Spell her name?
Is it Tracey with an
E before the y?
Or Tracy
without the e?

The mother's brow
Furrows as if she is
Trying to remember
Her PIN number.
—Jus' a minute.

She rolls up her sleeve
And looks at her arm,
Her mouth moving
Silently as she
Studies the tattoo.
Then she shows her
Forearm to the teacher
Who says,
—Ok, that will be Traci
With a small i

Social Worker Story

The social worker
Was from Holland.
She had learned
English for the job;
She spoke it perfectly.

Unfortunately
Her placement was
In the Medway Towns.

She asked the boy:
—Do you have
   Many friends?
—Godfree.

—Is Godfrey your best friend?
—Oo miss?

—Godfrey.
—Oo miss?

—You said Godfrey
   Is your friend.
—Oo miss?

—I asked if you had
   Many friends and
   you said Godfrey.

—I sed, I. God. Free. Frens.
Free! Like it's a number, innit?

North Kent English Lesson

Listen and repeat: *ka oon* equals cartoon.
Tah oo equals tattoo and *buh er* is butter.

It is *Margit* not Margate and you do not
Go to the PENTAGON shopping centre but

To *der pen agin shopin sen er.*
Don't worry you will get the hang of it.

Remember it's no good resorting to
Oxbridge English here or shouting

At people as if they are deaf. In the worst
Case scenario this may result in you

Being fed a Chatham delicacy known
As a *knuckle sandwich* AKA a *bunch of fives.*

We are not to be confused with
Cockneys although they, like us, have

A glottal stop, but we also clip our words
At the end as well as in the middle.

Darren, Wayne and Tracy are guilty as
Charged of taking your words without

Consent but like it or not this is not illegal.
They took them on a joy ride and left

The body burnt out in a field outside of
Rochester, having first removed the radio.

We *chored* some *kushti* words from the
Romani, *chored* them as easy as £2.50
Worth of ham from *SAFEWAY* on a quiet

Wednesday afternoon when the
Security guard was on his tea break.

Chatham 1987

woodsmoke icecream

Indian Summer
neither one thing

nor another.

septemberfire.
octoberheat.

clear sky at night.

woodsmokeicecream.

Two Skinheads On Chatham Hill

These two lads walking down
Chatham Hill and under the dirty
Brown brick mouth of Luton Arches,
Into Chatham High Street.
Both are wearing *Crombie* coats,
Ben Sherman shirts and
Sporting skinhead haircuts.
They could be identical twins.
Their *Doc Martins* splashing
In puddles as they stomp along
One says to the other,
—Where you goin'?
The other replies,
—Up Berlin
—Up Berlin?
—Yeah, up Berlin
—Ow're you getting there?
—Bus
—Bus?
—Where you fink it is?
—Dunno…up norf somewhere
sin it in a war film. Lots of
Bombed buildings and
Dead soldiers. Smart!
His mate sneers and says,
—Well it ain't up Birmingham
is it? you fick barstid!
The man walking behind them
Does not think anyone will
Believe this exchange
But he writes it down anyway.

Overheard by Billy Childish 1982

Chatham High Street, April 1982

Behind me
In the crowd
I hear a woman
Shouting at
Someone,
YOU'VE
GOT A FACE
LIKE A
SMACKED ARSE!
I look around
And see this
Bloke whose
Face is like a
Fist holding
A cigarette
Between thumb
And index finger.
She screams at
Him as he
Keeps walking
Away from her,
His expression
Punching a hole
Through the
Middle of
Saturday
Afternoon and
Halfway into
Next week.

Bhangra Music

A car passes,
Bhangra blares
From its stereo.
In the streets
Of Medway and
Gravesend
Rap meets Raga.
Bhangra blares
From the ride,
Bass cranked up.
In the passenger
Seat a young man
In a yellow turban
Says something
To the driver and
The car slows
To a crawl
As it passes
The corner shop.
Behind the counter
Armajit pauses
From painting
Her damson lidded
Eyes with kohl.
She hears the
Bhangra before
She sees the car.
The young man
Smiles and
Armajit also
Smiles a shy
Sly smile.
Her father stops
Stacking the cans
Of spaghetti hoops
And glares daggers

At the car and
And says,
Hatcha, must they
Have their music
So loud?
The boys see
The father and
The car gathers speed.

Chatham 1987

Urban Soul Retrieval Poem

Scalpels of ice and abuse
Have cut you from home.
Fathers and false friends
Drove you away from you.
But I have sent my helper
To bring you back.
Follow the city fox,
he is my *fetch.*
He will lead you down the
Narrow passages of the night,
Those alleyways that stink
Of cats and curries gone by,
Across the rubbish dumps
Of the mind where old fears
Lie like damp mattresses.
He will lead you
across car parks
Where rainbows dissolve
In black puddles and sodium
Lamps turn his red fur to gray.
He will lead you through
The restless boundaries
Of Cardboard City, where
People are beaten by the
Violence of homelessness.
He will lead you through the
Grids of housing estates,
Where TVs flicker in empty rooms.
Trust the city fox,
he is my *fetch.*

His feet run to the beat
Of my drum but he's not tame.
He only works with me
Because I don't pretend
To be a Shaman and promise
Never to put advertisements
In New Age magazines
Sandwiched between
Atlantean astrology
And crystal capitalism.
He knows I'm just
An ordinary poet
Who makes friends with shadows.
The city fox
                    is my *fetch.*
His fur smells of rain and summer
His feet run to the beat of
My drum but his heart is his own.
The city fox lives in the
Green dimension that is my
Unkempt back garden.
Let his wildness lead you to
My back door which is unlocked.
I've just made fresh coffee
And its aroma fills the kitchen.

1994

Peckish Poet

The block of flats looked like
A wedge of Battenberg Cake.

The setting sun was like
A plum tomato burst in a frying pan.

Note to self*: in future do not*
Start writing a poem when hungry.

This haiku has too many syllabubs.

Brick Trains

On a hill
In a town
Of hills,
We stand
And survey
Row upon
Row of
Terraced
Houses that
Seem like
Red brick
Railway trains,
Shunting
Up one
Impossible
Hillside
And down
The next;
Only to
Rise again
On another
Even steeper
Slope; as if
Under the
Enchantment
Of some
Sisyphus-style
Curse.

Chatham 1983

Lack of Self Knowledge Poem

The dog knows it should be
A wolf but cannot be one.

The human thinks he should be
An angel but he shouldn't.

The dog thinks the master is
An alpha wolf but he isn't.

The human thinks he is a devil
But he is only acting.

The tame cat thinks it is a
hunter but it isn't.

The politician thinks he is
honest but he isn't.

The racist thinks he is a
liberal but he isn't.

The man thinks he is a
feminist but he isn't.

The woman thinks she is not
sexist but she is.

The person reading a newspaper
Thinks he thinks but he doesn't.

Humans think they are human
And sometimes they are.

Wounds

String your guitar
With my hair.
Find a willow,
Hang me there;
          Saint Sebastianised
By the arrows
Of your lust.
You are my
Firing squad,
Your bed is a
Horizontal wall,
You offer me
A blindfold or
A last cigarette.
My navel holds
          a Ruby of devastation.
My nipples are
As hard as bullets.
My breasts are
Nails in the palms
Of your hands.

1999

Desire

I want to visit the
Ghetto warehouse,
Where the moon
Is kept, tied like
A great glowing
Helium balloon
Amongst crates
Containing citrus fruit
And Biblical tracts,
Guarded and
Maintained by
Secret grandfathers
In night stained kaftans.
I want you to teach me
To speak French
Like an African.
To hunt puma in the
Suburbs of the world.
To open up your
Box of desire and
Touch the tortured
Starfish that writhes
Between your legs.
To read the type
Off the page of
Every forbidden book.
To add and subtract
Your sacred gematria.
Most of all, I
Want to visit the
Ghetto warehouse,

Where the moon
Is kept, some night
When it's dark and
Judaic and scented
With ink and lemons.

1984

She Bathed In The Black Mirror

She bathed in the black mirror.
When she emerged
She was transparent and you could
See her clothes through her body.

Graffiti

When the job
Starts to numb
His mind

He skives in
The staff toilet.

He reads the wall
That says ten
Million flies
Can't be wrong.

I woz ere 1/2/68
I woz ere 3/6/68
I woz ere 10/6/69
I woz ere 3/12/70
I woz ere 8/5/71
I woz ere 7/5/72
I woz ere 6/6/ 73
I woz ere 9/ 8/ 74
I woz ere 8/ 9/ 74
I woz ere 3/6/ 75
I woz ere
I Woz,
I BLOODY
WELL WOZ!

1975

Winter

Ghosts on the dark side of the moon
Know your secret name.

Someone told me your mother was a
Yenta; a star; a piano.

You are on a first name basis with
Rumpelstiltskin and your hair

Is straw spun from gold; one winter
When freezing fog was on the hill

Like the veil on the face of a bride,
I kissed your cold lips and they tasted blue.

1979

The Joys of Living In Terraced Housing

The slamming
Of car doors
After midnight,
The gunning
Of engines.
The muffled
Throb of
Acid house,
Hip hop and
Techno jungle
Through the walls
The *effing*
And *blinding* of
Vicious innocents
On the roller-skated
Hop scotched
Pavement.
The flushing
Of cisterns
The switching
On and off of
Other people's
Central heating
Systems.
The chocolate brown
Cat with
Yellow eyes
Whose feet creak
On the PVC roof
Of our neighbour's
Extension until

It is hit by a
Thin strategically
Delivered jet
From the water pistol
I keep by the bed

Specifically for
That purpose.
Unfortunately the
Pistol only works
On disturbances
Of a feline nature.

1985

Winter Poem

In the winter of 1987, we
Heard on the local radio
That they needed volunteers
To dig out the Out Patients
Dept at All Saints Hospital.

We lived just around
The corner so we spent the
Morning shovelling snow,
It felt good, working up
A sweat and being useful.

Someone told me the plough
Being brought over from
Gillingham had overturned
            killing the driver.

Later that evening, we heard
A weather warning that
Sounded like a proverb:
When passing a snow blower
Beware of flying Catseyes.

Later on BBC News
I heard a doctor say:
            Hypothermia is just
The tip of the iceberg.

1987

Proof Read

Help, my text is being proof read
By foxes and crows dressed as
            cardinals and psychiatrists.

I write, the river *Styx:* S.T.Y.X.
But when it is fixed in hard copy
I read, the river *sticks:* S.T.I.C.K.S

Help, dog foxes and vixens are
Running through my sleep,
Scattering my unwritten works
                across the countryside.

Help, my life is being proof read
By shit stirrers and April foolers.

I am being badly dubbed.
I say, *I need you* but it comes out
I feed you and you hear *I bleed you.*

The Bodhran Player

for Aimée and Rory

Aimée's dad, a bodhran maker from
Orkney built her a drum as round as the
                    Ring of Brodgar.
A Neolithic heartbeat waiting to be woken.

Aimée filled it with weather and witches,
White horses and gull cries.
Her wrist is the lightning before the thunder.

Rory, her love, is a man made of music.
In their kitchen, spoons dance; cups and
Saucers become ceramic
                    percussion instruments;
The teapot is a timpani.
Their disagreements are as
                    syncopated as their loving.

HOSPITAL POEMS

Bill Lewis circa 1980

Theatre Story

His x-ray showed:
Pieces of light bulb,
Glass and filaments,
A rusty knife blade,
A fork and spoon,
A Half Hunter
Pocket watch,
Fob, chain and
Several nuts
                    and bolts.

In the recovery room
The theatre sister
Looked back and noticed
The small spanner on
The oxygen cylinder
Was missing and
He was smiling.

West Kent General 1979

Therapy Room

Joe's making a stool.
I'm weaving a basket.
Someone's making coffee.
Dee says, *I can sing.*
But she can't.
although she does.
Jane won't
Make an ashtray.
Arthur's sulking because
The hospital Padre
Wouldn't re-christen
Him *Jesus Christ.*
Jane still won't
Make an ashtray.
Instead she
Becomes a dog. *Grrrr*
Woof-Woof-Woof!
Because, she points out:
Dogs don't make ashtrays.
Which we all
Agree is true
Dee is singing the
National Anthem.
Arthur blesses me.
Sydney hasn't spoken
All morning or yesterday
Or the day before.
Grrrr Woof-Woof-Woof!
Shit, says Joe,
I'm going to discharge
Myself from this place.
It's driving me mad.
Realising what he
Has just said
He starts to laugh.
The man on my left
        (who didn't hear Joe)

Starts to laugh as well.
We all laugh.
Except Sid, who wants
To die (and means it).
Then we had coffee.

Crossfields Psychiatric Unit 1976

West Kent General Morning

A weary staff nurse,
Strand of hair escaping
Her white cap, clocks out
From her shift, opening
The door at the main
Entrance, allowing
Savlon yellow sunlight to
  stream into the corridor.

The only sounds are
The sci-fi hum of an
Electric polisher and
Somewhere a domestic
Whistling a hymn tune
That converts to a
Beatles song in the second
Verse but returns to
Sanctity by the coda.

1979

Casualty Story

This morning, in Casualty,
A young man ate a live pigeon

It flapped about as he bit into it,
Feathers and
          blood flying everywhere.

Nobody could stop him,
               although several tried.

The patient sitting next to him
                       vomited and the

Young policeman who had
          brought him in, fainted.

Ward Round. 5 Mini poems

1.
here
the pulse
is a
blip
of light
on a
circular
screen.

2.
On his
Lunch break
He practices
Micro-surgery.

Literally
Splitting
Hairs.

3.
In the canteen the
NUPE poster
Said: *REAL ANGELS HAVE TO EAT!*
It's true. There are two
At the next table
Eating chips and
Moaning about Matron.

Tomorrow we are
On strike.

4.
She said, it doesn't have
To be too sterile.
I replied, that's like saying
He's just a little dead.

One could lead to the other

5.
Lady
Macbeth
Should
Have
Used
Hibi Scrub.

West Kent General Hospital 1979/82

The Red Heifer

"A Biblical injunction called for the sacrifice of a blemish free red heifer whose ashes (mixed with water) were sprinkled over those contaminated through contact with the dead"

The Dictionary Of The Jewish Religion

Click, I clock out.
My shift at the hospital
Over for another day.
Click and a small tab
Of brown card floats
From the base of the
Blic machine to join
A small pile of its
Comrades on the floor.
Needs emptying says
The chap next to me.
Not my job I reply
Although he wasn't
Really speaking to me.

Click I clock off as
All over town people
Are clocking on to the
Graveyard shift.
A man in a white coat
Guides a portable
X-Ray machine down
The corridor. It hums
Dalek-like, as if it's
Full of electronic bees.
He gets halfway to the
Ward when a second
Man in a white coat
Walks up to him and says
In an almost whisper
Take it back; too late;
We lost him.

Click, I clock out.
It is already late and the
Hospital is shrouded
In the evening's
State registered darkness,
Like a cape of a
Night Sister.
Leaving the microcosm
Of the West Kent General.
I walk down streets
Already too full of ghosts.
Passing a pub where
Someone once broke
My nose in a fight;
An alleyway where
Tramps, like shabby
Vampires, drink their
Life blood from the
Necks of cider bottles.
Crossing a bridge
I once jumped off.
In this town held
In sorceries of weather,
I catch a bus like
I catch a cold.
Bring on the red heifer,
Cover me with ashes.
For today it is my mind
That has touched the dead.

Bleep

Bleep-bleep-bleep
A fast bleep means
It's an arrest.
Bleep-bleep-bleep
Fingers on buttons;
Receivers to ears.
Bleep-bleep-bleep
    —A cardiac in casualty,
Comes the tin foil voice.
White coats
Blow down the
Corridor like
The contents of
A washing line
In a gale force wind.
Bleep-bleep-bleep
In this game of tag,
The first one there
Is IT and gets to
Use the silver needle
Or crack a rib in the
Old adrenal struggle.

1979

Five Shaman Songs

Shaman Song

is this a dream
i'm dreaming
is this a dream
i'm dreaming
or am i only
dreaming i am
in a dream

is this a song
i'm singing
is this a song
i'm singing
or am i just a song
that is being sung

i'm dancing
with the word
the word is
like a wife
the word is like
a knife a healing
surgeon's knife

is this a stone
i'm skimming
is this a stone
i'm skimming
or am i just a stone
skimming on
the wave

1992

Icaro For A Spirit Airplane

Bzzzzzzzzz I can hear the buzz
The Spirit Airplane is coming
It comes from a strange aerodrome
At the far end of the Cosmos
Bzzzzzzzzz I can hear the buzz
It's still a long way off but I
Can make out the yellow and
Black markings on its fuselage
Bzzzzzzzzz I can hear the buzz
The Spirit Airplane is a big
Bumble bee bringing medicine
From its strange aerodrome
Which is a big beehive at the
Far end of the Cosmos
Bzzzzzzzzz I can hear the buzz
A big beehive beyond the source
Of the Amazon where once the
Conquistadors searched for their
Fountain of sweet decaying dreams
Bzzzzzzzzz I can hear the buzz
The Spirit Airplane is coming
Parachutes are falling
Bringing crates of medicine.

NorseChrist

oldodin shamanhorsed
yggdrasilhung ninedays
polestarred & pointzeroed
spearsided & allfathered
crossroaded ninedays
tripletrinitytied mosthigh
all at once runereceptive
christfused in christconfusion
mythmelded wyrdwelded
webcentred & spiderhorsed
crazyhorsed & visionquested
godsacrificed togodtobegod
climbsdown fromuphigh
readynow norsechrist
gododin christodin
yggdrasilhung ninedays
readynow runerich with
covenants & covens
power prisms readynow
bifrostbright & burning.

ritual song for ripping your face off

let's go
some place
& rip our
faces off
let's go
some place
& rip our
faces off
we'll go into
the park
& rip our
faces off
we'll go into
the dark
& rip our
faces off
let's go
someplace
& swap
some secret
identities
i'll show
you mine if
you show
me yours.
let's rip
off these
masks of meat
let's go
someplace
& rip our
faces off

you can bring
your dog
but you
have to
leave your
car in
the garage.

taking off your fur coat song

we are bears
we are bears

we are bears
we are bears

we are bears
we are bears

we are bears
we are bears

but some of us
are in disguise

horse drum

i beat the drum.
the drum is a horse.
i ride the horse
into the land of grief.

i am the god
who walks in the garden
vines bursting out of
my open mouth.
in me there is no
east or west,
there is no
north or south.

i beat the drum.
the drum is a horse.
i ride the horse
into the land of grief.

i am inspired
so I may in turn inspire.
this circle
must not be broken.
for if the imagination
should die
this world
would be unspoken.

i beat the drum.
the drum is a horse.
i ride horse
into the land of grief.
through
to the land of dreams.

TWO BEAR POEMS

Bears

For *winter* read: *death.*
Spring brings a
Resurrection of bears.

I drink their fierceness
In strong brown draughts
Of ursine ale and carry
Their meaning in my blood.

Tomorrow I'll awake
With a sore head but
Tonight I will dig with
My paws for the medicinal
Roots of stars buried
                    in the night sky.

Berserk, bright and upright,
I range beneath the
Northernmost heptad,
A constellation of
                        barley grains,
Corn silk and shining in
The fields of arctic space.

Big Fisherman

Big Fisherman.
No, not St. Peter.
This guy is the
Pope of the forest.
Pine trees are
His Vatican.

Salmon leaping
Upstream jump
Into a yawning
Cave of fur, full
Of stalactites
And stalagmites.

His tongue is a
Red carpet rolled
Out for honoured
And permanent guests.

Big Fisherman.
No, not St. Peter
This guy eats fish
Not only on Fridays
But any day he
Damn well pleases.

1992

THREE COYOTE POEMS

Coyote Poem: Grand Theft Auto

Something tricky in the cosmos.
Something with pointy ears,

Something with a long nose,
Something with a ragged tail,

Something that steals your chickens.
Something that hot wires your car.
I'm talking grand theft auto,
          I'm talking grand theft auto.

Something that drives a
Stolen *Thunderbird* across the
Red Martian desert of the new Mexico
Bad Lands and smiles at you from the
Glossy cover of *Arizona Highways.*

Something that runs over a
                    roadrunner on Route 66.
Beep beep now, you little bastard
                    I said beep beep now.

Bad Mouthing Coyote

Wolf says, *when I howl you know it's me*
You can hear the cold:
my howl is wolf-shaped
You know I've come looking
for other wolf-kind.
When I howl it's like a million years of
Snowfall stacked up against your back door.

Fox says, *when you hear my*
cough-like bark you know it's me
Crossing the long dark miles
To morning, across several counties.
That it is the one they call El Zorro in
Spanish and The Russet Hound in the
tongue of the Celts.
Many hunters dog my steps.
Many vixens and hungry cubs wait.
I sound like a fox and my cousin the wolf
sounds like a wolf.
We both agree on one thing and that's this:
Coyote never sounds like coyote.
Coyote always sounds like someone doing
bad coyote impressions.

Coyote and The White Folks

Coyote watches the pilgrims land.
He's been getting bored.
After ten thousand years the native
Population is wise to his tricks.

Fact is, he'd been too good at his
Profession. Done himself out of a job.

Here was fresh meat. Poultry at that.
What a bunch of turkeys they looked.
Coyote celebrates Thanksgiving.

Coyote invents the stock market.
Everyone falls for it.

Coyote teaches Custer military tactics
(*That can be the only explanation*).

Coyote writes scripts for soap operas.
Everyone says they're like real life.

Coyote writes scripts for real life.
Everyone says it's just like a soap opera.

Coyote works as a Spin Doctor, gets
A movie actor elected as President.

Coyote says, *I think it's going to be*
Quite a few years until my retirement.

1992

10 Fox Poems 1975-2005

The first time I ever saw a fox
It was nailed to a barn door
I don't remember the fox too well
But the door was dark green.

I asked the fox, *is this forest*
You are leading me through
a metaphorical one?

He looks back and said,
No, I think it's Oak.

An owl, said the fox, *is a bird*
That only exists in a poem.
As he said this
An owl flew over head.
Oh dear, he added, *you know*
What that means, don't you?

My father, shotgun broken for safety,
Points at the orange ghost at the tree line,

See, he says, *see how he looks back*
Before he goes on? If he didn't do that

He would always be running.

★

His fur was russet trimmed with white.
His nose was long and sharp and his eyes
Were nightshade berry bright.
Cocking his head to one side like a dog
Trying to understand something it
couldn't quite fathom.
Then he asked, *why do you look like me?*

The medieval French word for fox was *Goupil*,
but because the Reynard poems
were so popular they changed it to
Reynard
a personal name.
It's like calling a species
Jack or *Jill.*

Reynard wonders why he has
Four legs but his shadow only has two.

★

There are things a poet should know, said the fox:
1) It is always later than it actually is and
2) Never let a dog help you with a jigsaw puzzle.

White letters on a white page.
poets, said the fox,
trace them in black.

The fox writes his autograph
In the snow with
a flourish of his brush.

1975-2003

Nine Haiku (1976-2003)

Racoons raid porch, get into everything
Through the bug screen: black masks.

Ghost Bears. Not Albinos. Product of
a recessive gene. Snow hidden.

The soul of the child is silver,
Mountain bike shaped, with 24 gears.

Bird beak beats tree bark
for juicy tasty grubs.
Woodpecker percussion.

Pyrenees, crystal crunch of snow.
No light pollution. Blizzard of stars.

★

By the fig tree trickster god has fun
With snake glove puppet in garden.

Out of seven years bad luck
you can create a flawless mirror.

It's the evening and the gardener holds
a portable rain shower

El Lobo’s nose:
an aroma map of scent trails.
Better than
Google Earth.

The Pre-History of Genetic Engineering

The Ice Age bit down hard.
Game was scarce so the
Wolves helped the humans
To hunt and then hung around
Afterwards for their share.
A man threw one of the wolves
Some cooked meat and the
Wolf entered his magnetic
Influence; a quadruped planet
Orbiting a bipedal star.
The man said, *trust me* and
The wolf woke up in the
Body of a Dachshund, in
The form of a Chihuahua.
Fetch the stick. Fetch the stick.
Moral: never trust anyone
Who walks on two legs.
They'll make you look stupid.

1990

The Truth Is A Traitor

Truth is a traitor.
It is not partisan
Nor a lover of
Ideologies.
It looks good
In any colour.
Often starting
With a revolution
It can defect to
The counter
revolution,
But return to the
Fold on the eve
Of the final battle.
It can walk from
One side of
The House
To the other
Mid debate and
Pass through
Walls like a ghost.
The truth is
Ambidextrous
And colour blind.
Truth is a traitor.

1979

Ann

Your eyes hold the
Warm quiet dark

Of sleeping books
Waiting to be read.

1980

Jaca

Passing the barracks at Jaca,
Ann looked out of the car window

and saw,
in the commandant's garden,
A young guardsman,

automatic pistol
in his hip holster
Submachine gun
slung over one shoulder,

as he pruned a rose bush.

Jaca, Spain, 1983

If I Were A Mirror

You say you are not beautiful
But that is because the only time

You see yourself is when
You are scowling into a mirror.

You don’t see yourself when you
Look at me and smile.

If I were a mirror you would
See a beautiful woman.

2005

Dear You

You must try to love *you* more than you do.
Not the you trapped in the prison of bone.
But the bit of you that exists in all others.

Nature does not hate itself. Babies are born as I write
And white hot blossoms of stars grow outward.
Nature does not hate itself even when hunting and
Feeding off itself;
so why should you?

Drink deep the sacramental wine of whirling galaxies
And wild suns. Sing songs with saints and
Scientists beneath the synagogue of the sky
Love nature and remember that the nearest bit
of nature to you *is* you.

Bright Garbage

Cities abused by a misuse of light.
Crew cut lawns lit all night long.

Suburban gardens have become
An extension of the living room;

Neat nature for the anal retentive.
Buffer states annexed by the ego.

A squandering of hydroelectricity,
An arc of golden light
pissed against the wall.

In the 1980's they said,
you are what you own.

By the end of that decade it was:
you are what you throw away.

Our lives are the Cola can,
Two sips taken then left to go flat.

We are the apple, one bite missing,
tossed into the gutter.

We are the fresh loaf discarded in
The bin before it has even
hit the supermarket shelf.

1992

Amnesia

There are many kinds of amnesia.

The forced amnesia of the conquered
The convenient amnesia of the conqueror.

The filed under *A* amnesia of the bureaucrat.

The spiritual amnesia of the consumer.
The sexual amnesia of the impotent.

The marine amnesia of the new born.
The defensive amnesia of the abused.

The youthful amnesia of the innocent.
The childlike amnesia of the senile.

There are many kinds of amnesia.
So many, that I have forgotten most of them.

2003

Avelino and The Gringuita Archaeologist

Night, and the green and hungry stars
Bleed their avocado rays upon the bed
Where the *Gringuita* dreams of Avelino,
the foreman on the dig.
She found herself watching him at odd
Moments during the long blistering day,
Finding it hard to concentrate on labelling
Artefacts; and at noon he had peeled an
Orange, using the two foot long blade
Of his machete as if it were a penknife,
Offering her its thirst-quenching segments.
Last year at *Chichen Itza* he had swapped
Mayan lessons for English. When not
Working for archaeologists he toiled in
The fields, or in road gangs for dirt wages.

Night, and the green and hungry stars
Bleed their avocado rays and she tosses
And turns, reliving that machete moment.
Now she sees him examining not an
Orange, but the Sun to see if it is ripe
Enough for her to eat, his Luna face
Broad and beaming beneath the jagged
Rim of his beat-up panama. Suddenly he
Plucks the solar orb from the sky and
With one flashing sweep cuts it in two
Splitting light into a thousand wet colours,
Myriad pigments that soak into her
White cotton dress like spilt fruit juice.

Mercedes

Mercedes Sosa
present personification of
Pachamama
Voice big enough to hold
to rock
the entire population of
America Latina
in a cradle of sound
(duerme duerme negrito)
singing us *samba,*
milonga, ranchero, son y jazz
y cha cha cha.
Your drum
tu bomba
the heart of the world
and the audience also
like a great
HEART
leaping out
To be with you
in time and in history with you.

Royal Festival Hall 1999

Juanita

(for Julie Felix and Joan Baez)

Juanita, the crystal blackbird
Has flown to you again
As she does each day at dawn
From the top-most perch
In the bending perfumed
Branches of the guitar tree.
Maybe that's how you see
Beyond the purple tents of the
Circus of sorrows, where the
Clowns of death are falling like
Playing cards in the wind.

Juanita, you are riding the
Big yellow school bus of
Civil disobedience beneath
The meteor showers of August.
The blood-stained jacket of the
Dead black prophet draped
Over your shoulders like justice.

Juanita, the crystal blackbird
Has come to live in the soft
Cage of your throat, so when
You sing both voices intermingle.
So now we too can hear what you
See from the swaying limb-like
branches of the guitar tree.
The billion bright tomorrows
Of the grandchildren of the sun.

Popular Mechanics

thou deep wet ache
at the centre of a
spiral galaxy
thou dark red itch
at the centre of the
deep wet ache
at the centre of a
spiral galaxy
thou long wet stab
that tries but fails
to reach the
dark red itch
at the centre of the
deep wet ache
at the centre of a
spiral galaxy
thou warm moist
spasm that tries
but can't quite
snatch the long
wet stab that tries
but fails to
reach the dark red
itch at the centre
of the deep wet
ache at the centre
of a spiral galaxy
oh itch oh ache
oh deep oh wet
oh stab oh snatch
oh oh oh oh

You Are Not On The Good Green Road

You know when you are not
On the good green road,
When the forest rushes past
And only the highway matters.

You know when you are not
On the good green road,
When you turn off the radio
And silence bangs knitting
Needles into your ear drums.

You know you are lost when
You start to believe the road
        is a symbol for the map;

When, unlike some Celtic saint
No grassy bank rises up at your
                back to protect you.

You know when you are not
On the good green road when,
Like blue half remembered
Dreams, the mountains keep
Their distance no matter how
Fast you hurtle towards them.

1993

Light And The Ley Hunter

I am amazed by the magnetic maze of miles.
The long span of the Long Man's reach.

Sunwise and widdershinned by well and way
Those sainted springs of water, power and

Will, bubbling to break the surface and spill
And spell the winding worm within the hill.

The silver trails and labyrinthine shell upon
The druid dodman's back. In the Toddman's

Horsewhispering west, where rest the smith
Shoed bones of amphibian sacrifices made

When Cole was king and 3 fiddlers called.
I fell like a shower of hazel nuts into the pool

Where the salmon of wisdom fed. When old
Father Horn first raised his blood stiff club

To the sky, I lay down to rest like a compass
On a map. Wet grass at my back and the stars

Tracing ley lines upon the terrestrial globes of
My eyes; my sight looks back to where tachyon

Particles play, back beyond the Big Bang, where
Eternity with a geomancer's art, joins dot to dot

Upon the open puzzle book of my imagination.

Blodeuwedd

Both ninth wave and ninth particle,
I am a quantum mechanics of
flowers and feathers.
I am made negative or positive
by the politics of fashion.
My thighs are bronze age riddles
That whisper as I walk at a pitch
only lovers and poets perceive,
Like a warning of seven
notches cut into birch bark.
I am a duality of alphabets
in constant flight and flux,
tree ogham
/bird ogham
bird ogham
/tree ogham
Sap sings in my belly
warm as a nest of down.
I, Blodeuwedd, am clothed in the
Long memory of the bluebell,
On this dawn of owl pellet grey,
When women and men embrace trees
to protect them from
bulldozers and earthmovers.

1993

Shadow Warrior

It's only me, the idiot boy, I'm here
Beating down the door of your
University with the butt of my rifle.
I've come to liberate those libraries
Where I was not
                    eligible for a reader's card.
Now I turn paper to fire and read my
Biography in the residue of white ash.
I clap my hands and the bright bow ties
At the throats of college professors
Turn into deaths-head moths.
Oh Universities of dreaming
                    liars and scheming spires,
I need to crack open the skulls of
Descartes' disciples to see if their
Heads are really full of clockwork.
Oh Universities bereft of creative
Intellectuals but packed with pedantic
Academics, be of good cheer I've
Come to save you from mediocrity.
I've been training for this for 200 years
In these green and pleasant hills.
With rods and pendulums I sought out
Allies beneath the grass and now the
Tribes of Gog and Magog are with me.
I ride the *White Horse Of Uffington.*
The Green Knight rides at my elbow.
His axe is thirsty for the beheading game
I have decorated the barrel of my rifle
With the feathers of fish eagles found
In the long barrows
               of paleolithic ancestors

My face is blue with woad and my
Nom de guerre is, *War Dog.*
On my shield is an endless knot.
I have trained for this for 200 years
In these green and pleasant hills.
The mills and factories are closed;
The coal mines redundant;
Now it is your turn to welcome me.

Holy War

My imaginary
                friend
Is better
      than yours!

2005

Shadow Dog

I always feed my
Shadow dog
But not too much.
If he was overweight
He would blot
Out the sun.
I let him run free
In the night park
Where the moon dial
Marks the hour.
Though I always
Keep him on a lead
In residential areas.
I never wear
His collar
And let him take
Me for a walk.
If I did that he would
Drag me across fields
Of muddy miles
Where PRIVATE PROPERTY
KEEP OUT signs
Stand guard.
He'd bury me
In the garden
Like an old bone
And then forget
Where he put me.
I pat his eclipse colored
Head and never
On any occasion
Keep him cooped up
In the house.
If I ignored him
Like that he would
Most certainly bite me.

Bee Sting

When lies
Are said in
Anger they

Sound like
The truth.

You are stung.

I am a
Dying bee.

Ants

look down
there at
those
armies of
full stops
in deep
canyons
carrying
grass stalks
and twigs
up to
3 times
bigger than
themselves

in deep
canyons
taking slaves
farming
aphids
filling larders
freezers
petrol tanks
buying tvs
microwave
ovens and
VCR recorders
cup cakes
waffles
deodorants
tupperware
trainers
haute couture
clothes
with cool
logos

in deep
canyons

once the
marriage
is over
she loses
her wings

soon after
mating, the
male dies

1984

With Jung In Africa

He was fast becoming his own archetype
A wizard dressed in misty tweeds.
As the red wind blew across
the Serengeti plain,
Piping a tune on the river reeds.
All of a sudden you can lose yourself
In the heat and the dust and the flies.
All of a sudden the *Jungfrau* was gone
And *Kilimanjaro* filled his eyes.
The river reeds became a papyrus book.
A scroll as curved as time and space.
He started to unfurl its fabric and
Found he was in a deep dark place.
Dreaming awake in the desert night.
Head on a pillow, as cool as stone.
A ladder of selves extends from him
Its base stands in a cave of bone.
A trail of numbers that are letters;
Breadcrumbs scattered by a dancing god.
Here a *Yod* here a *Heh* here a *Vah*
Dragged into being by a primal *Yod.*
Hold the writing to her lips of glass
Say an anti-clockwise Gnostic prayer.
See the future hiding in the past
as if lit by a solar flare.
I'll let you touch my burning bush
If you trust your fingers to the fire
He stares into the polished sand, screaming
YOU'RE A LIAR.
I'll give you the fountain pen
Of youth with its platinum nib.
If you peel off your ghost white shirt
and replace my missing rib.

His heart is a burnished anchor.
His mind a merchant ship.
He wrestles with an angel
                                        and dislocates a hip.
The red wind blew the Martian dust
Giving him a pseudo tan,
And what was lost was found again,
In the sacred song of the Hippo Man.

Blackberry Ghosts

for Robert Holdstock

We rode the hedgerow horses
As far as the edge woods.
As I look back today, through
A coppiced memory and feel
Again the weight of a basket,
Afternoon heavy with dark
Clusters of vitamin stars,
Wrists and arms patterned
With bramble scratches.
Ritual exchanges of blood
For fruit seemed fair enough
To us kids; our hands stained,
Remaining dark long after our
Mouths lost their memory.
I ride again, the hedgerow horses
As far as the edge woods
But no further, for at the
Rim of a Green Hole
Time distortions abound.
In the bracken my foot finds
A rusty pre-ring-pull can
Opened by a *church-key* in the
Hands of a pre-teenager who I
Hope in turn was opened by life.
Blackberry ghosts crowd the
Periphery of my vision and
Though I stand stock still, a lighter,
Faster version of myself,
A Chalk Boy from an abandoned
Earth Work, is travelling the
Wents and *Hollowings,* intent on
Finding a breach in the impenetrable
Oak vortices, an oscillating traverse
Leading to an uncoppiced past.

Glass Harmonica Blues

You are a glass harmonica.
Full of the smoke and spit of
                    human existence.

You wear your coat of rain.
It has a black river in its lining.
It wraps around you like suicide.

I remember when you always
Had a bottle zipped tight under
Your black leather jacket,
Just to keep your ribs cool,
Purely for medicinal purposes.

I watched you build bonfires of
Expensive musical instruments,
National guitars internationalized,
Blazing pianos and violated violas.

1977

360°

The circle has turned 360°
Silver; green; silver;
and soon, silver again.
Just as all things turn
however wild their orbits.
Our own home world turns,
Held in place by
the unconditional love
That keeps all things together;
That wears many masks
From Newton's law of gravity
To Einstein's
Space-Time Continuum.

Our Mother is part of a
Greater turning,
a steering wheel of stars
Held by the strong hands
of magnetic force.

Buddha said, *the only*
constant thing is
change.
The book of the Tao is called
I CHING:
The Book Of Changes.

We have learned to confuse
consistency with stagnancy.

The Navajo call our mother:
Changing Woman.
She is a shape-shifter.
Changing Woman
Sleeps beneath a white blanket;
Dreams that the blanket is
Green; wakes up and it *is* green.

A Rosary For Maria Sabina

Woman constructed out of language.
Woman alphabetized by an Alpha
And Omega of mushrooms and weeds.
Woman whose flesh is a living codex.
An ethnobotanical lexicon woman.
Clock woman who claps a steady
Metronomic measure to her song,
Whose prayers are wrapped in a
Banana leaf like an aromatic *tamale.*
In the earth grow children and clowns
That make us laugh;
                                        we cry in our catharsis.
Primordial Clown woman, you know
That there is awe in our laughter,
That there is grief in our hilarity.
A Mazatec Christ crucified on a
Cruel cross of cactus, his blood is in the
Coffee crop, his body in the maize;
He shines like a Meso-American Apollo.
Hummingbird woman who sucks the
Sweet nectar of sickness out of my body.
Woman with a broom of herbs with
Which you sweep the nervous mountains.
Woman who is embroidered on the
Huipil of dawn in threads of mist.
Woman who moves a bead of bright
Sound upon the rosary of her tongue.
Woman whose tongue is a Bering Strait.
Woman whose tongue is a land bridge.
We cross it into the land of health
        We cross it into the land of health
                We cross it into the land of health

1994

The Blue House

In the blue house, Frida Kahlo rises through
Sheets of silver fever, her body bathed
In the platinum sweat of pneumonia.
In the blue house, the Left Handed Hummingbird
Caresses her body at the zenith of the
stepped pyramid of life.
The sun drinks the crimson pulque
Of her blood and is intoxicated;
Mexico will live another year and another.
But she is already carried free by four
jade green parrots, away from the
steel corset of time and space.
Above the canopy of her bed, sprawls
Judas Iscariot, fireworks strapped to his limbs.
He wears a mask of sugar,
his heart is an icicle.
In the blue house, her dress is a flag of hope.
Her untamed hair spreads like a puddle of
black water on the crisp pillow.
Revealing the votive hand hanging from the
miracle of her ear.
In the blue house all is quiet, except
For the paintings on the walls. Self portraits
Whose honesty renders us clairvoyant.
We read her every thought, for like the *Golem*
Life and death are written on her forehead.
In the studio, pigments are no longer mixed
As they are in the streets of Mexico City.
A wheelchair faces the easel where
Joseph Stalin stands unfinished
fireworks strapped to his limbs.
He wears a mask of sugar,
his heart is an ice pick.

In the blue house,
Like the white shadow of Christ, a deer
Leaps from the forest, its exquisite hide
scarred by arrows and amputations
That are nothing but
Unos cuantos piquetitos,
For one who has been carried free by
four jade green parrots.
On the wall of the blue house, under leaf dappled
Shadows, a plaque bears the inscription:
Frida and Diego lived in this house 1920-1954

1992

Sheela Na Gig

Wind-kissed are my tumuli.
Wet mud sucks your iron spade.

Anoint this nub of flesh
For it is the hub of my wheel.

It is the polar axis of the
Spinning palace of the year.

Caress this crevice of clay,
With agriculture and Archangels.

Rub the plough with fennel and
Incense, hallowed soap and salt.

Ride me with hobby horses and
Dig me with the archeology of

Your rain drenched desire.
Furrow me with antler picks.

Sow me with a semen of light,
The oyster ejaculations of dawn.

Mistletoe berries caught in a
Lifted apron of the finest linen.

I pull back the moss-moist labia,
And see the winter is pregnant

With the spring and spring has
Summer curled and fetal in her womb

And inside summer, autumn waits,
Dreaming in golden hibernation.

Mind Is Not The Brain Poem

My heart and my gut
Are engaged in a
Christian/Pagan dialogue.

My left brain is Marxist.
My right brain is Buddhist.

My hand makes decisions
My feet are unsure of,
Yet each have their own
Areas of expertise.

My body has adopted a
New management style.
It is a blame free culture.
My head is no longer
The boss but a facilitator.

We Drink From Each Other's Mouths

The goodbye hidden in the hello,
I am in you and you are in me.
The anchor sunk in your inland sea,
I am in you and you are in me.
Like a name buried in a place,
Or eternity hidden in a human face.
The shaft thrust into the thigh,
The sword pulled from the anvil.
The hardness beneath the silk,
The hook that lacerates the lip.
Like the purple crocus in the bulb,
The fire locked in the fossil fuel,
Like the singularity seen as dual.
Like the moon bred in the bone
And the iron colouring the blood,
Between the ascent and the descent,
Between the drought and the rain,
We drink from each other's mouths.

1999

Passport

The hand grenade does not
Study *Das Kapital.*

The machine gun is ignorant
Of its Capitalist fathers.

The *Uzi* semi automatic has
Never debated the *Talmud*

The ground to air missile has
Never read *The Holy Koran.*

Semtex has never reflected
On *The Synoptic Gospels.*

Radiation does not recognise
International borders.

It is its own passport.

1977

Is That Me In Your Poem?

People try to find themselves in my poems
I have a red dress just like that, is that me?

I'm blonde; I'm a redhead; I'm brunette;
I'm beautiful so it must be me, mustn't it?

But I wasn't in Paris with you or New York!
I never fired a Kalashnikov or walked on the moon!

When did I sit in that café with green walls
And share a black coffee with an angel?

A Unicorn never laid its head in my lap!

But it must be me because I did see you once
When it was raining and it was September.

It's a futile exercise. That woman was many
I knew or none. It might even have been me.

Watching Women

Watching the Hispanic woman on
The deck of the Staten Island Ferry
Eating pistachio nuts out of a
Brown paper bag, her tongue
Wriggling against her back
Teeth to dislodge fragments,
Her dark eyebrows
                    doing a bossa nova.
Or the tall black woman (*who*
May not *have been a woman*
But who cares, certainly not me)
On the Paris Metro, put down
Her/his copy of *Marie Claire*
And peeled an orange, her/his long
Mauve finger nails releasing
A fine spray of zest and the
Entire carriage becoming an
          underground orange grove.
Or you sitting opposite me
A moustache of cappuccino froth
On your upper lip, or the way
You unconsciously touch your
Hair after you have walked past
A man or a woman that you
Know is looking at you like
You are the best thing on the menu,
Never daring to look back and
See if they are still looking.
Watching you sleep, the tip of
Your tongue just visible between
Your teeth, your REM
Flickering beneath stretched lids.

Paperback City

There was geography piled everywhere;
Detectives on the stairs with names

Like *Nazi Gold* and *Magnum Murder;*
Stacks of Penguins with fractured spines;

Picadors unhorsed and unjacketed;
Dusty blue Pelicans speaking sociology,
Psychology (in fact all the *ologies).*

She asks, Is *Misery* good?
Yes, he replies, it's upstairs in the
Same place as the *Nausea* that you wanted.

One Hundred Years of Solitude is right at
The back of the shop under *Foreign.*

No, I haven't got *Laughter and Forgetting* but
I do have *An Unbearable Lightness of Being.*

1985

True True Blood Conversation

—I don't suppose you have any of her
other series?

—No just True Blood.

—I prefer her detective ones. To be honest
Vampires leave me cold

—Vampires are the new black.

2005

Love

love that is not dangerous is not really love that is not dangerous is not really

Touch

The blind finger
reads the Braille
of your body,
Charting constellations
of moles and freckles,
milk chocolate stars.
The blind finger
Feeling for the
flinch of welcome.
Tracing translucent
watermarks woven into
the forbidden text
of your skin.
Invisible tattoos.

1998

Bring Me The Moustache Of Gabriel Garcia Marquez

Bring me the moustache
Of Gabriel Garcia Marquez.

I last saw it being used as
A bookmark between the
Pages of an Isabel Allende.

I'm rereading Don Quixote.
And if I don't mark the place,
I am sure the text will change
        each time I put it down.

        I need a special kind
Of bookmark because
I'm rereading Don Quixote
And I am not the same person
As I was when I last read it.

1989

Everyone Should Have Their Own Bridge In Paris

Ann said, Look, right over there is where in
That movie *Charade* Audrey Hepburn said
To Cary Grant, *Right over there is where*
Leslie Caron danced with Gene Kelly in
An American In Paris.

One day somebody not yet born may read
This poem and be walking by this bridge
And say, That's where Ann Lewis in that
Poem by her husband said,
Look, right over there is where in
That movie *Charade* Audrey Hepburn said
To Cary Grant, *Right over there is where*
Leslie Caron danced with Gene Kelly in
An American In Paris.

That same somebody as yet unborn may
Think it fun to add their bit to this poem.

Paris 1989

Beauty Is The Beast

Ask the ape on
The Empire State.

Ask the mantis
Husband or the
Arachnid mate.

Ask the star crossed
Kids of Verona.

Ask the Merchants
Of Venus behind
The beaded curtain
Of Soho sweat.

Ask the stick insect
Girls savaged
By fashion who
Will soon be the
Child brides of Death.

In all of its
Skin deep glory,
Beauty *is* the Beast.

2000

Green Men

Green Men grin and gurn
From blackened beams,
That creak and groan as
Ancient houses dream;
Swayed by wind in
Branches long since snapped.
Foliate faces flower in the
Memory of an antique hour,
Unwinding beneath a
carpenter's craft;
Masons also saw their shape
Sleeping in the stone.
So all is forest then:
Vegetable, mineral,
flesh and bone.
The World Tree becomes
The column of my spine,
Eyelids: leaves of Oak.
Fingers: Ash and Pine.
I am lost within a wood
That is lost within me.
Green Men grin and gurn,
For no one knows more
Than they what is and is not tree.

Rochester Cathedral 1994

The Green Man

Break
through
this petrified logic.
Speak of the
bio-degradable art
of the forest floor,
where matter
breaks down,
where life is recycled
In mould and mulch.
Neither the vanity
of kings and bishops,
of theologians and politicians
could hold you
in its stone strait jacket.
You are that which cannot be contained.
Our minds are cathedrals
dreaming they are forests.
Our stone faces crack;
we are coshed by chemicals,
fastened by fashions and therapies.
But just as old leaves
are turned into new forests
every breakdown, in its green alchemy,
if recognised,
should
be a
break
through.

Gypsy

Again I find myself walking a crooked mile.
Down a road of dead names with four stolen
Nails in my pocket, antique and Galilean,
Planted on me by the Gadje police.
They are an even bigger blood libel than that
Laid against the door steps of the Jews.
Because of them the Inquisition did not
Even extend the option of conversion.
Because of them they nailed our hats to our heads.

My name is Maleva and I keep a photo
Of Lon Chaney junior wrapped in
Tissue paper and wolf bane beneath my bed.
I tell the fair headed children that my son
Bela has a pentacle in the palm of his hand.

My name is Esmerelda and a French priest
Flays my skin with his gaze, like a spiritual
Hunchback caught in the amber mirror of my
wolf eyes.
My captain is the sun, I am a *rawnee* of power.
In you I inspire operas but not compassion.

My name is Petrolengro, my birth certificate
Is an oak tree at a crossroads in Andalusia.
All of my *chavvies* are *kushti* and I pin
Heather to your sleep with a *be-lucky-luv*
to ward off the devil and his dog.

1978

It Hurts So Good To Be Alive

Don’t take this
Pain away.

It’s mine not yours.
I have a right to it.

It is like the outline
Of a body that can

No longer be touched,

A missing smile that

Nobody ever
  bothered to photograph.

So hands off, I own it.

Don’t take this
Pain away

Don’t give me
Morphine or *ganja,*

Mood elevators or
Mood depressors,

Red wine or religion,
Revolution or whisky,

Tobacco or therapy
Flowers or
Feel-good movies,

This is my pain.
I own it.

It hurts so good.

It hurts so good
To be.

It hurts so good
To be alive.

Five Haiku (2003-2005)

Sleep: and I am carrying a heavy wardrobe
across a ploughed field.

The monkey on my back was hungry
and ate the chip on my shoulder.

An analogy: Something poets get
when the pollen count is high.

Is that a haiku in your pocket
or are you just pleased to see me?

In your hot damp little kitchen
I lick Thai fish sauce from my finger.

Saint Oscar Of The Americas

Archbishop Oscar Romero
Pleaded with the armed forces
Of El Salvador, asking them
Not to kill their peasant brothers
And sisters, saying that:
                    the poor are Christ.
He was later gunned down as he
Celebrated Mass, his blood
Mixing with the bread and wine
On the church floor, in a savage
Reaffirmation of the sacrament.

Somewhere a factory wall is
Spray canned *Jesus Christ*
        Greatest LIVING revolutionary.

Down the dark passage of
History a burning graffiti fish
Swims in a sea of stone.

1987

Then I Am Praying

If I recite
A poem and
The audience
Suddenly
Realise
It is they,
Not I, who
Wrote it.
Then I
Am praying.

If, during
A strike,
I take my
Place on the
Picket line
And someone
Spits in my
Face and
Verbally
Abuses me,
And I look
Into their
Eyes and see
Not an
Enemy but
A different
Kind of
Victim,
Then I am
Praying.

May my
Voice beat
Against the
Riot shield
Harder than
Any stone.

1979

Earth Mass: The Bread of Recognition

"The meaning of all corn is wheat, and of all
metals: gold, and of all births that of humanity"
—Meister Eckhart

Ears of barley hear silent prayers.
Whole bread is made of broken corn.

When bread is broken we see this
And we know the spirituality of the whole
That is made out of the broken

Then the loaf becomes the bread of recognition
Because not only do we see this
But we see ourselves made whole by our
brokenness.

For we are the bread of paradox,
Broken and whole together, and though
We know it we do not know we know it
Until we see ourselves in the bread.

All bread is holy, it is sanctified
By the rain and the sun and the starving
Peoples of the Earth, and needs no words
Of blessing by any priest to make it so.

Earth Mass: The Wine of Connecting

Clouds the size
Of countries.

The fertile clefts
Or river valleys

and ninety-three million miles
of solar light packed
into the skin
of every
grape,

Liberated by the press
And poured into a cask.

Taste the rainfall of
A whole year and the
South facing slopes
Of lost memories;

The alchemical embrace of
The earth's clay oven;

Be connected to the vine
By the wine of
Interconnectedness.

The Hands Of The Poor Are Maps Of Heaven

The hands of the poor
Are maps of heaven.
Horn hard the
Upturned palms.
Each scar that
Breaks the lines
Of life and Venus,
Is a testimony
To the plough
And the stubborn dirt.
Cross them with
Silver seeds,
The title deeds
Of land reform
And the irrigation
Ditches of
Everlasting waters.
The hands of
The poor are
Maps of heaven,
That also record the
The voyages of the rich.

1987

Uilleann Pipes

for Martha Mckeever

u
ul
ulu
ulul
ululating
an ul
lulating
green landscape
of sound
and grass crowned
in the peat-deep dark
beneath your feet
six hundred kings and
secret commonwealths of smoke
lay in the embrace of
deep green sleep
beneath your naked feet
and the blessed
bodhran beaten earth
beneath your bee-droned and en
chanted chanter
oh ul ul lu ul ul lu
oh ul ul
ululating
undulating
uilleann
pipes
ulul
ulu
ul
u

Cleaners

I keep ripping my head off
Says Vi, and her ciggie, glued
To her bottom lip, bobs
Up and down as she talks.

That's the second time I've
Pulled it off this morning.

I keep getting it stuck under a
Gondola and when I yank it out
It comes off every time.

And as for this Hoover
Says Vi, *it ain't got enough blow*
To suck the hairs off mi pussy.

1993

The 164

Crammed onto the
164 as it trundles up
Magpie Hall Road

Sardine tight amongst
BO, bad breath
And baby buggies.

A beer can rolls about
As the bus climbs
The steep gradient

A woman sitting
Behind me remarks
To her companion:
Today my voice hurts.

Today she also spoke
The very stuff of poetry.

I Am The Stone That Breaks All Hearts

I am the stone
That breaks
Every heart.

I am the stone
In the flesh
Of your cherry.

I am the stone
In the shoe of
Your pilgrimage;
The dried pulse,
The irritant
Beneath the
Mattress of your
Sleeplessness.

I am the stone.
Scatterer of crows.

I am the stone
Left unturned.

I am the stone
Broken by windows.

I am the stone
Left unthrown
In the house of glass.

I am the stone
That breaks all hearts.

THE AMERICAS

A War Of Flowers

for Claribel and Bud

In another America where
The memory is a war of flowers.
Behind the curtain of silence,
Rests a grey heat heavier than iron.
Where the red jaguar reclines
And the blue tiger of prophecy
Smashes the world to bits
With a mighty war club of
Lilies and golden orchids.
Shattering the night and using
The shards of its darkness to
Reconstruct the morning,
Luminous with lakes
                                        and lepidoptera.
Devalued are the old currencies
Of chocolate and emerald feathers.
A steel cough hacks at our
External lungs: the trees.
The General crushes a gardenia
In the palm of his leather glove.
The Cardinal blesses birdcages,
Brass bands, baseball games and
Endless parades of paper petals.
The memory is a war of flowers,
A bloody war of flowers.
In another America where
The helicopter gun-ship desecrates
The azure robe of the mountains.
Where the only *mariachis* are
Orchestras of skeletons playing
Their rib cages like *marimbas.*

Nicaragua 1989

Inca Moonshot

The good ship *Santa Maria* dry docks in a
Dry bay by a dry Sea of Tranquillity,
Having first, without knowing it, cleared the
Sensuous curve of the Earth's gentle hip and
Fallen into the here-be-dragons-dark
of black airless history.
Captain Christopher Columbus still thinks
he has reached the coast of Cathay.

He scans the horizon with a brass telescope,
Not realising he is looking down the wrong
End; he sees in the distance, like angels cut
From tin foil, blonde blue eyed astronauts
Rounding off a game of golf. Behind them on a
flag pole *Old Glory* unflutters in a windless sky.

Neither the sea captain nor the *gringo* space men
Realise that they were not
the first to venture here.
Long before the invention of the sailing ship,
Long before all the Apollo missions,
The people of the under developed world
Walked the Lunar surface by the
sacred technology
Of song, dream and visions, or simply
by calling her Grandmother.
They left no footprints, they walked lightly
(as they did upon the Earth).
They took no part in the Space Race, in which
The USA and the USSR jointly held last place.

1992

Drive-In, New York State 1992

Greg, our American host, suggested
we take in a drive-in movie,
A vanishing bit of Americana.
Drive-in banks and fast food
Are on the increase but not movies.
We get there too late to get speakers
So we have to tune our car radio
Into the sound track. There are three
Screens, showing *Batman 2, Pinocchio*
And the one we are watching,
A League Of Their Own, a picture about
An all woman baseball team in the 1940's,
Starring Madonna.
We tune into
The wrong sound track and Pinocchio's
Voice comes out of Madonna's mouth:
There are no strings to hold me down/
To make me smile, to make me frown/
There are no strings on me/
We laugh; eat hot dogs; sip cold beer.
The night smells of pine needles and home fries.
The family next to us sit on an old settee
They've rigged up on the back of
Their pickup. Mom, Dad and three kids
All wearing identical baseball caps,
Hands like mechanical diggers
Excavating large tubs of pop corn.
Unusually for me, my attention wanders
From the film, to the woods beyond
The screen where glowing clouds of
Fireflies dance in the dark,
little miracles of bio-luminosity.

The Entry Of Christ Into The USA

In the wide smile of Rigoberta Menchú
I see *mucha gente, mucha gente en Dios.*

Los Americanos, del norte y del sur.
I say *del norte*
Y del sur
Because America is much more than the USA.
It is a prophecy of
pluralistic power as yet unfulfilled.
Today I see with the rainbow clarity
of a *muralista:*
all the christs.
The anonymous christs of
countless communities.
Christs born before and after
Jesus of Nazareth.
All the copper coloured christs of Fr. Peyote.
The *café con leché* christs of the *favelas.*
The blue black mood-indigo santeria christs
Whose song was born in the
wooden womb of the slave ship,
Arriba Changó, arriba Changó
arriba Changó, arriba Changó, señores!
A sidewalk splashed with libations of spiced
golden rum and offerings of Havana cigars.
While up above, on the skyscrapers over the
Avenue of the Americas,
up near the cloud lodge of the
Sky Chief,
Mohawk steeplejacks in yellow fibreglass hardhats,
dance across steel girders
with the grace of a deer.
Today I see with the rainbow clarity of a
muralista,
all the christs, some of them not Christian
just as Jesus of Nazareth *wasn't* Christian.

Los Americanos del norte
your christ is on welfare
and living in the Projects.
Los Americanos del norte,
your christ is on the Reservation
and a recovering alchoholic
Los Americanos del norte,
your christ is an illegal,
crossing the Rio Grande of your
conscience at night.
Christ is a wetback, don't send him back.
Why not let her teach you to
habla español a little,
let him teach you to mambo.
let her teach you how
to create more and consume less.
This christ hasn't come to form a church
Just as Jesus of Nazareth didn't.
He wants to show you the Christology
of the broken tortilla;
the parable of the roasted dove
and the assassinated president;
the theology of the guitar;
the socialism that existed before Marx
the democracy that
existed before Athens.
Today I see with the rainbow clarity of a
muralista,
The quetzalcoatl christ rises
in the wide smile of Rigoberta Menchú.

Halloween Headquarters U.S.A.

Bag-O-Fun Trash Bags assorted orange and black,
Best value at just eighty nine cents.
Single Jack-O-Lanterns, five feet tall,
Also three foot witches, ghosts and werewolves.

Remember, we are your Halloween Headquarters,
Just around the corner from the Food Hall.
You can find us situated between
Toys-R-Us and Dunkin DoNuts. *Open till midnight.*

It is Fall, west of the Forbidden Planet.
A plastic hand reaches out of the lawn.
The National Enquirer reports Killer Clowns.
The wind is as bitter as poisoned candy.

They've found the wreckage of a B-17 on the moon.
Alligators are breeding in the sewer system.
It's time for skull buckets and plastic pumpkin heads,
Styrofoam tombstones and gaping gargoyles.

The FBI declares war on the drug dealers.
The CIA run drugs to fund Nicaraguan Contras.
The game show host smiles like a razor blade
Hidden in the crisp corpse of a *winesap* apple.

In the monochrome of the Outer Limits, we can
Control your horizontal and vertical hold.
The blond serial killer with the Mormon smile
Composes blank verse in the Klingon language.

Remember, we are your Halloween Headquarters.
Bag-O-Fun Trash Bags assorted orange and black.
The seller of lightning rods has come to town,
Mummy dust and powdered moths fall from his shoes.

Rhode Island, USA, 1994

Dog Soldiers

A band of Cheyenne Dog Soldiers are being pursued by Federal troops. The Dog Soldiers will not surrender and the cavalry will not give up their pursuit. The Dog Soldiers realise this and ride their ponies into the sky. Once they are in the sky the Dog Soldiers turn themselves into stars. The Cavalry watch them twinkle in the heavens and realise they are beyond their reach. The Federal troops return to the fort. The captain decides not to report what happened to his superiors as magic is not covered by military protocols.

From the unpublished Book Of Sherds

Dirty Money

The woman next to her
In the ladies washroom
Of the Pequot Tribe's casino,

Furiously scrubs her hands and says,
Money sure is dirty!

This is said without
the slightest trace of irony.

The Jewish God Tells Jokes In The New York City Of Dreams

Like a *klutz* the night
Stumbles down back streets,
A *yekl* in an immigrant hat
And a sack full of hair and stars
Over his shoulder.
On the fire escape a young
Woman wearing a wedding dress
And sun glasses sings an ancient
Song about cigarettes, sung in
A minor key and in a language
Few but the dead can afford
To speak; although its syntax
Haunts every city on the
Eastern seaboard of the USA.

The groom wore a coat woven
Of seven days but it was too bright
For her and they separated
Soon after the ceremony.
In the hope of reconciliation
Their lawyers have arranged for
Them to meet only at weekends
By soft candle light.
Mazeltov!
The glass wrapped in a handkerchief
Unshatters beneath the heel.
Her garden has not been
Penetrated by time.

In a downstairs apartment
The old tailor dozes, a tape measure
Across his shoulder like
a prayer shawl,

His eyes blanket stitched with sleep.
Once a passing God reached into
His dreams and asked a riddle:
When is a sewing machine
Not a sewing machine?
Answer: When it's a *Singer.*
It was this painful pun that pulled
Him by the beard from the
Old country to be a stranger
In yet another strange land
Oy, such a God already he thinks
From this he makes a universe?

A New Dawn Over New Mexico

Like mummified bats
Ristras of dried chili peppers
Hang from the roof beams.
Against the red adobe of Old Town
The new
New Mexico dawn spreads,
Turning the whitewashed walls of the
El Vado motel—*continuous hospitality*
for over 55 years—pink.
We cross Route 66 to breakfast at the
VILLAGE INN
International House Of Pancakes,
the sky above
Albuquerque is full of
Angels *Saints*
Coyotes
dancing to the music of
silent accordions.
I like to listen to the way the old guys
At the next table switch from
English
to Spanish, often
mid—
sentence,
As natural as *eggs ranchero*
blueberry pancakes
and coffee.
A new New Mexico dawn with the
Sandía Mountains grinning like
Slices of rosé coloured watermelon.

Ghost Ranch

For Georgia O'Keefe

She was a cactus flower
That bloomed out there

In the bleach-bone white
Of the steer-skull day.

Where ice crystals formed
In impotent thunderheads

Evaporating long before
Rain could reach earth.

In this arid place she
Nurtured her fertile

Imagination much as the
Indigenous people farm

What seems to us a desert
And to them a garden.

1992

Storm Blanket

Storm blanket,
Spider woman
Spun fire fibre,
Breeze blown
Ox blood red
And ochre.
Called into creation
By howling
Canyon people
From deep
Within the limestone
Walls of sleep.
Blazing blue corn
And yellow
Dog dreams.
Dancing
            Petroglyphs.
Meteorite memories
Like the half
Recalled locations
Of lost gold mines
That inspire the
Pollen painted
Fingers, full
Of grace, of
Navajo madonnas.
Storm blanket,
Talking textile,
Campfire cloth,
Dyed in the wool
Yarns retold and
Rich in the retelling.
Rattlesnake go
Zigzagging
From my
Boot heel go
Zigzagging

From lilac lit
Cathedral clouds,
Over haunted mesas.
Beetles creep
Across branches
Bearing baskets
Of molten light.
Storm blanket
Burning as if
Woven from
Fibre optic thread.
Sacred software
Of a prehistoric
programme.
Storm blanket
I saw you there all
gracias a la vida vivid,
In a store front
On Main Street,
I saw you there
Spread in a
Window display,
A square of summer
Beneath a glacier
Of plate glass.
A visitation from
The world of creators,
In captivity in the
Land of consumers,
Where music is
An industry and
Art a commodity
Fixed with the
price tags
Of over abstraction.
I couldn't afford
You then at $600

But it is better
That I carry your
Priceless beauty
Forever in the
Eye of my breath.

New Mexico 1992

Tropical Fruit

If you
Treat
People
As if
They
Are
Manure
For your
Banana
Crop
They're
Going to
End up
Tossing
You a
Steel
Pineapple

Love In The Rainy Season

In the city of pirates, at the mouth
of the hidden river,
we lay with our heads close to
the electric fan
to stop our brains from frying.
We lay in a half sleep like the
sticky embrace of the
mythical thighs of mermaids.

We fashion houses of perspiration
and enter their rooms.
Before morning, we smoke
vanilla flavoured
cigarettes from across the border,
as the equatorial force of
the rain
machine guns the zinc roof;
We hear, or think we hear,
The termites of linear time
eating away the wooden townships
of the Atlantic coast.

Bluefields Nicaragua 1989

Traffic

Lady don't pay the coyote
The coyote always wants more,
He's doing his recalculations
When he thinks that
          you're not keeping score.

He'll carry you across the river.
He'll smuggle you across the sea.
But the border is inside of you
It's something you cannot see.

Expensive boots of Spanish leather.
A snakeskin band around his hat.
An army of *pistoleros* who
               keep the coyote fat.

The traffic is always heavy
On the highway of human flesh.
The desperation of the poor
               keeps the product fresh.

Some of you are going to make it.
Some will be sent back some day.
But some will disappear for good
Because they could not pay.

Lady don't pay the coyote.
The coyote he always wants more.
He's doing his recalculations
When he thinks that
          you're not keeping score.

Objects

The bloody door won't open.
He says, STUPID DOOR.
The door *is* stupid and I can see
                    that it is a bit thick.
The door is stupid. The windows
Blind and deaf. The car engine
A moron and neither the hammer
Nor the drill have a degree
From the University of Kent.
The train is late. The TV is
Disabled but with a lack of
Charity he thumps it anyway.
The telephone is being obtuse
          and the directory is dyslexic.
The can opener is psychotic and
Wants his blood and as for the
Microwave, that just stares at him
With dumb insolence while he
Beats up the kitchen and then
Moves on to the rest of the house.

1990

Fish Are The New Bicycles

Read it
In the *glossies:*
Pink is the
New black.
Saw it in
The *Sundays:*
Poetry is
The new
Rock n roll.
Heard it
On *BBC*
Breakfast TV:
Dressing up
Is the new
Dressing down.
Food is the
New sex,
The garden
Is the new
Kitchen.
What next?
Just wait,
Gay is the
New straight,
Geese are the
New dogs,
America is the
New Rome,
The office
Is the
New home,
Thai is the
New
Tex-Mex,
Text is the
New talk,

Seattle is the
New New York,
Cuba is the
New Spain
(Which is
Ironic as
It was part of
The old
New Spain.)
E is the
New cocaine,
Tapes are
The new
Books.
What next?
Feet are the
New hands,
Rats are the
New mice,
Fire is the
New ice,
Once is the
New twice.
It all happens,
I'm told,
In cycles.
Fish are the
New bicycles.

Men Are Electrical Appliances, Women Are Lamp Shades

In the Book Store,
I'm standing between
The *Misery Lit*
Section and *Self Help*
There are stacks of
Pop Psychology books,
Titles such as *Men Are*
From Mars, Women
Are From Venus.

Men Are Dogs
Women Are Cats.
Men Are Plugs
Women Are Sockets.
Men Are Greenhouses
Women Are Ironing Boards.
Men Are Electric Razors
Women Are Band Aids.
Men Are Carbonated
Mineral Water and
Women Are Still.
Men Are Electrical
Appliances And
Women Are Lamp Shades.

Why isn't there a
Book entitled
Some Women Are Men And
Some Men Are Women?

Or *Men And Women Are*
All People But Some Are
Nicer To Each Other
Than Others?

a) because this title is
far too long and

b) it does not propagate
conflict between genders
and back up glib
generalisations that
we all want to hear.

Fig

1.
She digs her fingers into
The flesh of the fig
Splitting it apart.
Showing it to the man
In all its glistening glory
Saying, *Does that*
Remind you of anything?

Oh god, he gasps.

Close, she says, *but*
You left off the e and
The double s.

2.
After they had finished
What the fruit had
Inspired in him,
And he lies snoring,
She thought to herself:
That wasn't as good as
I expected it to be.
Over so fast and
I'm still hungry.

She remembered how
That pretty snake
Had slithered over
Her legs and belly;

Those elastic hours
Of ecstasy that sweet
Serpent had given her.

But then, after all,
It was in its nature,
Being both brother *and*
Sister to the moon.

The man had been a very
Strong and muscular
Piece of prose but
The serpent had been poetry.

The Beast

The Beast sits by the telephone.
Beauty does not call anymore.

Outside across the lawn a peacock
Cries out like a woman being murdered.

The Beast sits inside, curtains block out
The garden where stone animals crowd.

The Beast wears an eye patch.
Beauty stabbed him in the eye

With the slim blade of her body.
Her smile is a Stanley knife.

The delicate lines around her mouth
Cut deep into his sight. His vision hurts.

She is not intentionally cruel but her face
Is a loaded gun that he presses against
The temple of his memory.

He is caught in a pincer movement,
His bad body image on one side,
Beauty on the other.

He reads Angela Carter novels, fairy tales
And Mother Goose and hopes that wisdom
Does not go stale over the centuries.
In these stories she always returns.

To be honest he fears that a little.
He has, after all, only one eye left.

He plays records. It is the nature of
The Beast to own vinyl, not a CD collection.
Julie London cries him a river.
Frank Sinatra sings: *it can happen to you/*
Fairy tales can come true.

He does not know that sentimentality
Is an act of violence.

In the dark bedroom, his good eye waters.

1998

Shapeshifting

1)
Beyond the
  POLICE LINE DO NOT CROSS
Tape,
On the tarmac
The outline
Of my body in
White chalk.
The actual
Cadaver has
Been removed
From the
Crime scene.
The shape of
My limbs bent
In an uncomfortable
Position as if
Frozen in some
Ecstatic and
Exotic dance.
My prone image
Stark under
The flashbulbs of
Naked City
Photographers.
There are eight
Million stories
In this city
And I am just
One of them.
I am wearing
One red shoe
The other is
Several inches
Away from my
Right foot
Or where my

Right foot was
Before I
Was moved.
It begins to rain
The chalk
Outline blurs
Then dissolves.
I am undone.

2)
She said
It's like this:
You remember
That TV show
Back in
The Sixties,
The Prisoner.
Each week over
The credits
His captor
Would say,
I am Number Two.
The Prisoner
Would ask,
Who is Number One?
But Number Two
Never answered
Instead he'd say
You are Number Six.
The Prisoner
Would shout
I am not
A number
I am a free man!
At the end
Of the series,
When he tries
To escape,
He confronts

What appears
To be
Number One.
He pulls
Off his mask.
Underneath is
Another mask.
A gorilla face.
Monkey laughter.
The Prisoner
Pulls off
That mask
As well and
Finds his
Own face
Looking back
At him.
Remember?
Well that's
How it is.
That's how it
Always is.
Yoda tells
Luke Skywalker,
To go into
That dark place,
That cave
Under the
Roots of
A tree.
Remember?
He tells the
Young hero
That he must
Not take anything
With him.
No weapons.
No defence
Mechanisms.

Down there,
Under there,
He meets
Darth Vader.
Light Sabres
Appear in
Their hands.
They fight.
Luke cuts
Darth Vader's
Head off and
It rolls across
The floor.
It turns into
Luke's head,
Then vanishes.
You can't kill
The Shadow.
It's part
Of you.

I remember
A Christian friend,
Asking me about
The Shadow.
After I had
Explained
What it was
He said, *But*
That's the bit
Of me that
I want to
Get rid off.
You can't,
I said,
Who is it in
Your Mythology
Who doesn't
Cast a shadow?

One of the
Ways we become
Devils is by
Trying to
Eradicate the
Evil in us.

3)
I heard
Her voice
As I died to
This world,
As the rain
Washed away
My outline.
She said
It's a dance
Of masks,
It's like Joseph Campbell
Told us,
        Remember?
Eternity is
A hook
And we hang
A mask on it
To remind us
Where it is
But instead
Of entering
Eternity we
End up
Worshipping
The mask.
We call the
Mask God,
Goddess,
Buddha,
Yahweh,
Krishna,

Mammon,
Megaton,
Lightyear,
Luna,
The Company,
The Party,
The State,
The People,
The Power,
The Glory,
The Way,
The Truth,
The Light.

4)
Every Sacrament is
A door
Into the
Sacred but
Beware.
It is a
Revolving
Door,
That can
Spin you
Back into
The street,
In a worse
State than
When you
Entered.
Every sacrament
Can be a
Powerful
And addictive
Drug.
Tobacco,
Wine,
Sex.

Remove
The mask
From the hook,
Wear it
And look
Through
The eyes.
You think
Time is linear?
That you
Are born at A
And die at B?
Between those
Points I hope
That you look
Through the
Mask just once.
Once you are
In Eternity
You are always
There
Because
Eternity is…
Well….
Eternal.

5)
She said,
I know you.
A cross dresser
Double crossed
By your
Own body.
The Lone Wolf
Who, when
The pack
Is out hunting,
Stays behind
And dresses up

As a sheep
And looks
In the mirror.
I shave my body
But my shadow
Remains hairy.

6)
The good animals
Glue me
Back together.
At the end
Of a tunnel
Of smoke
I can hear
The *shaman*
Calling my name,
Calling me
Back
To the place
Of the living.
Just before I go
I'm shown
Something.
I'm looking up
From the surface
Of a river.
There is a child
On the river bank
Eating an
Ice cream.
The child is me.
I'm told
By a voice
In my ear:
The water rats
Thought you
Should see this.
Then I return.

My Father's Watch

Just before he died my father gave me his pocket watch. He always wore it looped through his waistcoat on a chain. It was made of alchemical gold, the kind that can change the colour of your soul. When my father died the watch disappeared. I found out later my mother had sold it to get money for cigarettes. I did not see the watch until thirty years later. In January 2000 a fox brought me the watch in his mouth. He will not give it to me. He wants to play. I must chase him. I have to catch him to prove to him that the watch is really mine.

If I see a dead fox by the side of the road I always get out of the car and check to see if there is a gold watch and chain in his mouth. You never know.

From The Book of Misplaced But Imperishable Names 2003

Cathode Ray Seahorse

My father is dead and my mother just sits in front of the TV most days smoking. Her eyes are the colour of denim that has been washed too often. He was probably the nearest she ever got to loving anyone. She lives for cigarettes and television. Today the TV set is on the blink. The screen keeps flashing but something strange is happening some of those flashes are in colour and our set is a black and white. This is very strange. My mother tells me to fix it but I know nothing of the workings of television sets. I try turning the horizontal and vertical knobs on the back. Another flash of colour zigzags across the screen. Then it happens. Something flies out of the screen into the room, an electric blue seahorse. It flies around the room as if our living room was a giant aquarium. *Catch it*, my mother yells, but it is up too high. *Go and get Rob's Dad he's tall,* she says. I run up North Street as fast as I can. *Oh, I seem to be a child again, how did that happen?* I explain to Mr. Earl about the seahorse. He returns with me, bringing a large butterfly net. The thought of him owning such a thing is almost as strange as the seahorse. When we arrive, the seahorse is flying around the room in circles and my mother is still watching the screen. The black and white TV is still flashing streaks of colour. I wonder what will fly out of it next. Then I notice it. The TV is not plugged in. This is just a dream. The seahorse deflates with a rasp like a dying balloon. My mother's eyes are shining like cigarette coupons. I wake up; I am an adult; both my parents are gone; they both died decades ago; my eyes are wet the way they are when I wake from UFO dreams.

The Cockroach Spoon

She is Spanish. Her husband is English. She tries to teach him Spanish. He decides to visit her parents in Madrid. Sitting in the kitchen with his mother-in-law, his wife's sisters and aunts, he tries to keep up with their rapid conversation. His mother-in-law sets a cup of coffee in front of him. He looks around for a spoon. There isn't one. He tries to remember the Spanish word for spoon. He thinks he knows it. He asks for a spoon. The room goes quiet. Everyone is staring at him. The Spanish word for spoon is *La Cuchara*. However, he has asked for *La Cucaracha*: a cockroach. They stare at the Englishman who wants to stir his coffee with a cockroach.

From The Book Of Misplaced But Imperishable Names 2003

The Twentieth Century # 1

The three bears come back from their walk. They live in a neat little cottage in *The Wild Wood,* which used to be *very* wild but now it's a nice neat suburban housing estate and everything is much tidier. They are horrified to discover their house has been burgled. Porridge has been eaten; furniture broken; beds slept in.

Baby Bear finds a semi-comatose blonde in his bed. He sniffs her. She smells of booze and by her dishevelled appearance he thinks she may have had sex. Much worse than this, someone had placed Modern Art in the centre of the room and you can't move without tripping over it. Father Bear is getting angry.

'You'd better take a look outside', says Mother Bear.

Father Bear goes out into the garden. His mouth drops open in disbelief. This is the final straw! Someone, some vandal, has placed a very large Twentieth Century in the middle of the nice neat lawn.

'Who is responsible for this outrage?'

A man steps out of the shadows.

'It was I', says Pablo Picasso, 'and I am not sorry."

From The Book Of Misplaced But Imperishable Names 2003

The Twentieth Century # 2:
Listen With The Eyes Of The Heart

The Maestro Joaquín Rodrigo was born in the first year of the 20th Century. At the age of three he went blind but here is the paradox: The Maestro's music is full of pictures. People who have never been to Spain close their eyes when listening to his compositions and say to themselves, ah España, and they see Rodrigo's country. They see the plains of La Mancha strung with white windmills; the plaza mayor at Salamanca in the late afternoon, when the golden light kisses the walls that are veined red with iron; the spire of a cathedral rising above a field of sunflowers, always with one of them turning its face from the sun like a heretic from the church.

The eyes in Rodrigo's head are dim but the eyes of his heart can still see. Pepé Romero says, 'the Maestro has paid a price for his genius. Often, he has woken in the night in great distress, not knowing who he is. *Who am I, Pepé? I don't know who I am.* I pick up a guitar and I play a piece of his music, perhaps the *Concierto de Aranjuez*, and I say, this is who you are, Maestro, this is who you are.'

I am not a genius like Joaquín Rodrigo. Nor are my eyes blind, although I don't always see what is important. But like him, I do wake in the night not knowing who I am. I blink into the blackness and I listen. But I have not written anything that anyone could play to me to tell me who I am. So, I listen. I listen to the distant barking of a dog. I listen for the shriek of an owl. I listen and I know one thing that the night is curved in the way scientists tell us time and space is curved. Curved like the naked back of a woman. I listen for the sound of a shadow falling on a sundial.

I listen for the sound of a flower opening in a distant garden where it is already dawn, where fountains and birds disguise themselves as the string and woodwind sections of an orchestra.

From The Book Of Misplaced But Imperishable Names 2003

The French Poet And The Shadow Of Her Shadow

A French poet once fell in love with the shadow of a woman's shadow. Yes, that's right, you heard me correctly: not the woman or her shadow but the shadow of her shadow. Poets are like that sometimes. I found this poet sleeping under marble in Montparnasse. It was too late to ask him about the woman or her shadow's shadow. A pilgrim had spelled out his name in small stones upon his bed. I believe later a song writer borrowed the shadow and put it into a great song of sad departures. The poet is gone. The song writer is gone. The woman is gone. Her shadow is gone, of course; but the shadow of her shadow? No that's still here living in his poem.

From the unpublished Book of Sherds

Borrowed Childhood

You lent me your childhood. It was happier than mine and now I remember some of it better than my own. But I have to say that I didn't look after it very well. I bent the pages back and the spine snapped; I placed coffee cups on its cover which left sticky ring marks; I even turned down the corner of pages; something I would never do to a book. You can have it back now.

From The Book Of Misplaced But Imperishable Names 2003

Crow Meets the New Neighbours

A crow, seeing he had new neighbours, flew down and told them how they should look after the land. The people who had lived there before understood him perfectly, but these new ones only heard *caw caw caw* and ignored him.

The crow told the eagle and the raven. They said, *maybe they are deaf.*

That is what the birds thought for a long while but when they saw how these new ones were behaving they changed their opinion. Raven said, *they stuff their fingers in their ears.* Eagle added, *and sometimes bits of plastic.*

The crow said, *no, not deaf, they are just stupid.*

From the unpublished Book of Sherds

Six Minutes And Nineteen Seconds

I want to tell you about this nearly perfect six minutes and nineteen seconds, which would have *been* perfect if you had been with me. It's a week-day afternoon, near the end of the week. Through the window, butter yellow sunlight. The Venetian blinds are making stripes on the wall. I'm drinking fresh ground coffee and listening to the *Romanza* from *Concertino para guitarra y orquesta la menor* by Salvador Bacarisse. There is a slight breeze playing with the wind chimes. The only other sounds are the blackbird who is the uncrowned king of my herb garden, informing his subjects that he still reigns, and the occasional faint buzz from the bees that are in love with the French Lavender by the wall and have their nest under the flat roof of the bathroom. The sound I would have liked to have heard are the heels of your shoes on the tiled floor of the kitchen. The moment lasts six minutes and nineteen seconds, then the music stops. You are not here so I wrote it down. Perhaps if, when you read this, you can feel as if you *were* here, we can join the two halves together and it *will* be perfect. If not, what good is writing?

From The Book Of Misplaced But Imperishable Names 2003

Acknowledgements

The black and white images in this book are all by me.

Thanks to those people who have taken photographs of me over the years which I have used in this book, especially Gloria Bousfield and Martin Wackenier (www.devine-timesphotography.com) and for Olivia Clark for helping with the proof reading. The cover was beautifully painted by hand (including the lettering) by Simon Mills (simonmills-artist.co.uk) who recreated my Bear Shaman picture from a print.

Special thanks to Ann Welch, Matt Fray, Sarah and Aidan Hehir, for their support for this project, and Simon Mills and Bronach Rae of the Colony Press for making this possible and keeping me sane through the process. Special thanks to Miles and Rachel at The Choir Press for putting up with all of my technical questions and for ironing out problems with typesetting and formatting. A special thanks to Ann for sharing the journey with me for almost four decades.

I really have the best friends that it is possible to have.

Biographical Note

Bill Lewis was a founder member of The Medway Poets and one of the thirteen founder members of The Stuckist Art Movement. He is also a member of Colony: A Community of Artists.

Lewis was appointed Writer-in-Residence for the Brighton Festival in 1985. He has performed his poetry in Nicaragua, the USA, France, Germany and his native UK. Lewis' work has been broadcast in the USA, UK and Australia and on Radio Faribundo Marti in El Salvador. He was winner of the Literature Award at The Medway Culture and Design Awards 2012 which was awarded for his contribution to the community and for his work mentoring new writers and artists.

He has been published in numerous magazines, journals and anthologies including *The Green Man* which won the world fantasy award, *The Grandchildren of Albion* edited by Michael Horowitz, *The Best Horror and Fantasy* edited by Terri Windling and Ellen Datlow, *Endicott Studios; Journal of Mythic Arts (USA), Poetry South East, The Collins Book of New Christian Verse, Beyond Bedlam (ed. Ken Smith), Rivers of Life (ed. Richard Berengarten), The Scarpefoot Zone, Social Work Today, Psychology Today, Bizarre Angel, Keep Newcastle Weird (New Zealand), Global Tapestry, Bogg, International Times, Critical Quarterly (ed. Cheryl Moskowitz), Ore, Iron, Slugs, Gazunder, The Cheapo Review, Smoke, Stand, Wormwood Review (USA), Junge Welt (Germany), Scarecrollective (Paris, France), Confluence, WOW Kent.* His work has been translated into Spanish, French, German and Farsi and his previous two books, *In The House Of Ladders* and *The Long Ago And Eternal Now* were published by Greenheart Press and are available from all good bookstores.

For more information please visit: www.billlewis-art.co.uk. or Wikipedia (Bill Lewis Poet, Medway Poets, Stuckism). You can also follow him on Twitter @BillLewis_Poet and on his Facebook Artist page BillLewisArts.

Rochester, 2016.

www.ingramcontent.com/pod-product-compliance
Ingram Content Group UK Ltd.
Pitfield, Milton Keynes, MK11 3LW, UK
UKHW040604210726
13854UKWH00009B/2696

9 781999 694807